GW00503274

STILL POINTS

Brother Richard is a priest-friar of the Irish branch of the Capuchin Franciscan order. For over 20 years, he has worked to bring the insights of the Christian contemplative tradition to greater public awareness, particularly with reference to modern mindfulness theory.

He holds honours degrees in philosophy, theology and English literature and also has post-graduate qualifications in pastoral and holistic studies and Franciscan spirituality and formation.

Brother Richard served as director of youth ministry for the Irish Capuchins for over ten years and is one of the core Shekinah Youth Retreat Ministry training programme developers.

He has also worked in hospital and prison relief chaplaincy roles and in parish work.

He was guardian and director of the Ards Friary and Retreat Centre in Donegal for three years and is currently working and ministering in Dublin.

With the Sanctuary Spirituality Centre in Dublin he has created many of the youth- and teacher-training programmes offered there as well as programmes based on the Christian contemplative tradition. His previous books include:

I Can Feel My Toes Breathe: Introducing Meditation to Young People with Niamh Bruce (co-author)

The Sanctuary Mindful Warrior Training Manual

Cave of the Heart: Meditations from the Christian Contemplative Tradition (audio)

The Four Inner Directions of Contemplation (audio)

A Day of Meditation and Reflection on the Ancient Desert Tradition (audio)

His poem 'Lockdown', reflecting on the early experience of the Covid-19 pandemic, went viral and was featured by both the BBC and CNN as well as being translated into over 26 languages, inspiring two short films and a number of pieces of music.

STILL POINTS

A Guide to Living the Mindful,

Meditative Way

Brother Richard OFM Cap

HACHETTE
BOOKS
IRELAND

First published in Ireland in 2022 by
HACHETTE BOOKS IRELAND

1

Cataloguing in Publication Data is available from the British Library

Extract from *Full Catastrophe Living, Revised Edition:*
How to Cope with Stress, Pain and Illness Using Mindfulness Meditation
by Jon Kabat-Zinn © 1990, 2013 reproduced with permission of
Little Brown Book Group Limited and Penguin Random House.
'Lockdown' was first published in hard copy as part of
A 21st Century Plague: Poetry from a Pandemic edited by Elayne Clift,
University Professors Press, US. 2021.

ISBN: 9781399700665

Set in 11.5pt Sabon
Book design and typesetting: Anú Design
Printed and bound by Clays Ltd, Elcograf, S.p.A

Hachette Books Ireland policy is to use papers that are natural, renewable and
recyclable products and made from wood grown in sustainable forests. The logging
and manufacturing processes are expected to conform to the environmental
regulations of the country of origin.

Hachette Books Ireland
8 Castlecourt Centre, Castleknock, Dublin 15, Ireland
A division of Hachette UK Ltd
Carmelite House, 50 Victoria Embankment, EC4Y 0DZ
www.hachettebooksireland.ie

To Mary, the woman of stillness,
she who is the solstice of the Lord

To the Little Sparrow of Assisi
and the Brothers and Sisters of the way

To the ancestors and the teachers and the Desert Rose

O Mary conceived without sin,
pray for us who have recourse to thee

Contents

Author's Note

This book is intended for anyone who wants to enter into the sacred stillness that is at the heart of all things and from which all that is arises. This stillness has many names, but, for Christians, entering this sacred place is always an encounter with the presence of God. For a few, this will be a return to a place of peace, well known and comfy like a favourite armchair. But, for most, as much as they may long for stillness, they know that to reach it often involves a battle with the distractions that are so present in our lives today.

It is my hope that the poems, still points, sacred pauses, meditations, practices and essays contained herein may act as telephone poles along your journey or oases that refresh and renew while supporting the message of love that runs in your breath as the background music to creation itself and to your own life.

This book may be used to follow the months of the year on a journey of discovery or it can be a book to dip into when the distractions arise or when you simply wish for an entry point, a still point in your day, to usher you into a deep connection to sacred stillness and the Divine Presence. You may discover sacred pauses or meditations that speak to you intimately at different points in your life. When you invite Divine Presence into your life with awareness and attention, then you can always trust that you will find what you need, when you need it, after you begin to practise sacred stillness. Each day, I would suggest sitting with and repeating the still point for that week and practising the daily meditation for 10 minutes a day, building up to 20 if that's possible.

I offer the poems, prayers and meditations in this book as the fruits of my own engagement with the contemplative tradition at the heart of the Franciscan vision of the gospel life. May they allow you to touch the still point at the heart of it all, the place where love abides, and help you to know the ordinary miracle of the present moment when lived in the presence of that love.

The Mindful,
Meditative Way

'Mindfulness' is the buzzword of the moment. It seems to be everywhere.

From psychology to education, from psychotherapy to the worlds of business and management, the 'mindful way of doing things' is often touted in many self-help books and seminars as the way to achieve happiness and success. This current wave of mindfulness arises primarily from the work of Dr Jon Kabat-Zinn, an American professor who, with his book *Full Catastrophe Living*, offered a way of becoming present to ourselves, to each other and to the transcendent dimension of life in a way that is accessible to everyone. He defines mindfulness as 'an awareness that arises through paying attention, on purpose, in the present moment, non-judgementally'. His work opened up the practice of secular mindfulness for the 20th century, and, of course, meditation. The aim of being fully present in the moment is a discipline that is historically associated with eastern traditions, such as Buddhism and Hinduism; however, all religions and cultures have taught that the mindful state is the prerequisite for beginning the meditative path, and this includes both the Jewish and Christian traditions.

Since Old Testament times, mindfulness – or attentiveness of the heart, which is known as *kavannah* in Hebrew – has been taught as an essential practice on the way of prayer. The revelation of the Divine name to Moses as he encounters the burning bush invites the chosen people into a unique awareness of God as the 'I AM', literally the only one who is truly present, who truly *is* and whose presence is accessed through deepening our awareness of his presence in every succeeding present moment. The ancient Jews taught that unless the law, the Torah, was observed with *kavannah*, then it could not be said to be observed truly.

> *Keep this book of the law always on your lips, meditate on it day and night, so that you may be careful to do everything written in it* (Joshua 1:8).

> *… and again, I will meditate on your precepts and fix my eyes on your ways, I will delight in your statutes; I will not forget your word* (Psalm 119:15–16).

Jesus himself teaches the disciples to dwell in the present moment, having no care for tomorrow but trusting in the loving providence of the Father: *Therefore do not worry about tomorrow, for tomorrow will worry about itself. Each day has enough trouble of its own* (Matt 6:34). In teaching them of prayer He insists that they enter the inner room of their heart and there encounter the presence of the Father who is already there, present and waiting for us in the present moment. (Matt: 6:6 *But when you pray go to your inner room, close your door and pray to your Father who is in secret.*)

In speaking of the Holy Spirit, the life of God within them, Jesus teaches his followers to perceive the presence of the spirit as the breath of life (*pneuma*), and after his resurrection he breathes the Holy Spirit over them. The spirit as the holy breath (*agios pneumatikos* as it was known in the early church) and is both our way into the awareness of the Divine Presence dwelling within us and the very means by which God calls us to this awareness.

The ancient Fathers of the church such as Sts John Climacus, John Cassian, Benedict, Gregory Nazianzus, and all those coming from the desert monastic tradition – those spiritual practitioners of the third to fifth centuries who went into the deserts of Egypt and Lebanon to seek uninterrupted awareness of God – continually spoke of the necessity of developing the 'art of attending to the present moment', being mindfully aware (*prosekai* in Greek), as the essential art of the man or woman who prays, and they developed many techniques for centring the mind in the heart through the use of the breath and the 'prayer word' (*versiculum*), so as to remain in this inner watchfulness in which the love of God may be truly encountered and then yielded to in such a way as to allow the Holy Spirit to begin his healing work of sanctification.

Over the succeeding centuries, many of the saints, mystics and great teachers of prayer have even spoken of the present moment as a 'sacramental space' in which, if we deepen our attention fully enough, become mindful enough, we will be able to discern the presence of God inviting us into contemplation and then hear the voice of God inviting us into mission. In modern times, saints and teachers – such as St Thérèse of Lisieux, Dom John Main, Thomas Merton, Abbot Thomas Keating and Pope St John Paul II – have all insisted that this contemplative, mindful dimension of Christianity must be taught once again as the birthright of all the baptised and so they have preached and taught its ancient way of practising the presence of God. Practices as seemingly diverse as *lectio divina* (the meditative reading of scripture); centring prayer (the practice of the presence of God); the Rosary; the Divine Mercy Chaplet; the Jesus Prayer; Eucharistic Adoration are all instruments that, when prayed with the attention of the heart, become ways by which we can encounter that deep stillness and silence that exists behind the noise of our distracting thoughts and allows us to *be still and know that I am God* (Psalm 46:10).

We can, therefore, safely say that the practice of mindfulness meditation, centred on Christ, has always been a part of our prayer tradition and we must give thanks that the modern wave of mindfulness has woken us up to the ever-ancient, ever-new contemplative path that is distinctively our own as Christians, while also giving us a space in which to dialogue with our brothers and sisters of other traditions and learn from them as they learn from us. The mindful, meditative path is the path of every Christian and indeed of every human being, and a universal invitation to know the God who *is* and whose '*is*ness of love' is revealed in the precious present moment.

As one of our own saintly brothers, Venerable Solanus Casey, always taught: 'All that God asks of humanity is that they be faithful to the present moment.'

Finding the Way
to Divine Presence

Over the centuries, this struggle to touch stillness and, through it to be ushered into Divine Presence, has resulted in our Christian tradition developing many ways to work with distraction, to deepen awareness and to grow in mindfulness of the Divine.

This has included the sanctifying of time and the seasons through ritual and deep attention and meditation so as to enter the present moment as a sacramental place of Divine Presence and revelation; the fruit of which is often the recognition that creation itself is a love letter to us from God, providing us with a gospel of truth and beauty to be read by all eyes and felt by all hearts. This practice of the presence of God, or the prayer of abiding in Divine Presence, is the uniquely Christian form of that which today is more readily known as 'mindfulness'. Throughout this book, I refer to Divine Love which is for us as Christians, the very essence of God (1 Jn 4:8) and to Divine Light which is the emanation of Divine Presence and the way that the presence is noticed in the heart.

A mindful Christian is one who, like any other practitioner of the way of attention, strives to live in the awareness of self, creation and the present moment. The difference with other forms of mindful practice is that we do this to be more fully aware of and awake to the presence of God who speaks to us in stillness and peace. 'Be still,' said the psalmist all those years ago, 'and you will know ...'

Blessings to you in this present moment.

Practical Advice
on Meditation

Over years of being taught the ways of meditative prayer by our brothers, many of them have shared a word of advice or teaching along the way. A few of them are recorded below; may they help you in your practice as they have helped me over the years.

1. Be regular in your practice; so far as is possible, practise at the same time and in the same place each day. You are a creature of habit. Let abiding in a state of prayer become habitual.

2. At the start meditate for 20 minutes, twice a day. If this is too much, begin with 10 minutes; better 10 with attention than 20 with struggle.

3. Begin with a formal gesture of invocation and an inner statement of intention, such as: 'I choose to be here and to enter with awareness the presence of God.'

4. Call on the heavenly helpers to assist you in your prayer. Your guardian angel, patron saints, holy ancestors and, above all, the Blessed Virgin want to assist you in your prayer, but they await your invitation.

5. End with a moment of thanksgiving.

6. Still yourself by noticing your senses and your breath. They are the gateways to the present moment.

7. Use a short phrase or word to anchor yourself in the moment of prayer. The 'prayer word' both unites us to God and gives the conceptual brain something to attend to until our thoughts quieten.

Some commonly used prayer words and phrases from our tradition include:

Abba! ('Father' in Aramaic)

maranatha ('Come, Lord' in Aramaic, the very last words of the Book of Revelation)

shalom ('Peace' in Hebrew)

Deus Meus et Omnia ('My God and my All' in Latin)

Kyrie Eleison, Christe Eleison ('Lord have mercy, Christ have mercy' in Greek)

veni, Sancte Spiritus ('Come, Holy Spirit' in Latin)

8. The prayer word or phrase should be in a language other than the one you speak daily as this will prevent associative ideas from arising and getting in the way.

9. Attend to your physical needs first, or you will just spend your time thinking about your needs.

10. Do not eat just before meditation. Your body is limited in its energy and eating beforehand draws necessary energy for the meditation to digestion instead.

11. Sit relaxed but with a straight back, let your breath be open and gentle without altering the rhythm in any way. As you become still, it will slow and deepen by itself.

12. Surrender all thoughts, images, sensations, concepts as they arise. Simply notice them but do not grasp them. Remain instead in simple attention attuned towards meeting the Divine Presence in this moment, in this breath.

13. Do not force anything.

14. Do not expect anything.

15. Try and meditate early in the morning as the sun rises and in the evening as it sets. In this way, you will be united with the natural rhythm of the cosmos and its Divine order.

16. You are just sitting, to sit. You are not owed anything. Anything you receive is a grace. Your job is just to show up, attend and be open.

17. The distractions are part of the process. With each return from the distraction, your faculty of attention will become stronger and your ability to maintain a centred awareness of the Divine Presence will grow.

18. Remember, God is already present within you and around you. You are simply tuning in to his presence.

19. There is nothing you can do to make God more present. There is much you can do to become more present to God.

20. Rest. You are loved. You are loved. You are loved.

21. In the end, this is not your work. You are being worked upon and within. You must simply turn up, abide past the distractions and attend to love's gaze.

22. Just close your eyes and get out of God's way.

Winter

Winter Beginnings

I spent a lot of my early life in the woods. The woods sang to me of presence, community, beauty and the transcendent Divine life from which they arose. They slowed me down and only revealed their miracles when I had learned the sacred lessons of stillness and solitude. Every day there held marvels and wonders that I was quick to soak up and learn with the sharp senses of childhood.

The season I have always loved the most – and this might seem surprising to some people – is winter. Naturally, from the human perspective we tend to think of winter as the ending of things. But if we look mindfully, with contemplative awareness, we find at its heart a new beginning. The landscape may look grey and empty – and the language we use to describe this season is often deathly and dark – and yet what seems lifeless is really pulsing with possibility for those who have enough awareness to see. Beneath the snow and frost, the land waits, the seed sleeps and the winter landscape guards the first green of spring until it is ready to appear again. All of winter is necessary for the spring to come. The snows and rain soak the land and are stored up in the roots to prepare for the first sap surge of tender-leaved growth. The cold breaks up the soil and allows the oxygen to circulate, stimulating the germination of the hidden seeds. The animal world rests, sleeps, gestates and readies itself for emergence at the right time.

The land teaches us that in every seeming ending is always the seed of beginning. As an elder brother taught me many years ago: 'An ending is simply a beginning seen through a veil of tears.'

So we begin this book not on New Year's Day when the world screams that you must be immediately a new person, perfect and resolute for a full year of improvement, instead – and at the pace of our own breath – we simply, gently begin with the turning of one year into another

As you read through this book, see its guidance through the still points of the year as an invitation to live in the depth dimension of your life; allow it to give you the gift we now call 'mindful awareness' but which in my tradition was simply known as spiritual recollection or, more actively, as the 'practice of the presence of God'. When we live consciously in mindful awareness, attentive to the movement of the spirit within and the divinely held beauty around us, we begin to realise that though there may be only one New Year's Day each year, there is an infinitude of new beginnings possible each day. Be still and you will know ...

Poem for the Fourth Day of January

Four days ago
you resolved to begin again;
and you did.
But so far today has been
difficult.
Don't worry.
Here is a secret that may help.
The trees do not know
that the new year has begun.
Neither does the mountain.
The stones keep their own deep time.
The first of January means little to the stars.
And even though the moon and sun
offer us the service of marking the days,
the months, the years, they
are not foolish enough to count them.
So you see, to begin or not
is your choice in every moment.
The river will continue its journey to the sea
whether you plunge in or not.
For today perhaps it is simply
necessary for you to sit beside it awhile
listening to its song of presence,
just knowing it is always ready for you
when you are ready to dive in again.
Let the cosmos teach you.
Before and after are always out of reach.
The calendar page is always falling away.
But every moment bears within it
the possibility of a new year, of a new life,

of a new you.
For every moment arises from
the Divine mind and heart, containing within
the breathing of the dove,
the fiery heart,
the origin of all,
the very ordering of creation,
the healing of all we find broken,
lost or yearning within.
So hear the call of the moment,
be open as the flower who,
not knowing nor asking
the time of her coming or going,
breathes deep and
simply blooms.

Meditation

Take time to think about some of the endings you have experienced in life. Notice the feelings that arise and will have your attention for a while. What do they want to teach you? Have you accepted their lessons yet? Sit with them, tend to them gently and with compassion as part of you, and then return to the present moment, anchoring yourself in your breath.

Breathing in: I accept the interplay of ending and beginning in my life.

Breathing out: I choose to practise beginning again in each moment.

Repeat this cycle for your meditation practice. If you become distracted, just gently return to the breath without any negative judgement or agitation.

January

They say that English is one of the worst languages to be a contemplative in! We take words and we nail meaning to them. We can see this especially in the little word 'love'. In English, it can mean anything from a simple liking ('I would love a cup of tea') to the very force that reveals the inner-heart longing of one for another ('I love you'). However, when we encounter Divine Love, we are entering the experience of the very essence of who and what God is. In the presence of Divine Love, we are abiding in the presence of the source of all being and the attentive, unconditional love that continues to hold all that is, ever was and ever will be in existence. For a Christian, contemplative Divine Love is infinite, unconditional and eternal. It is the source, the matrix of existence and the ultimate destination of all being, for *God is love* (1 John 4:8).

Week One

Still Point

In the Here and the Now

Why do you exist?
Here.
Now.
Out of the infinite possibilities in the mind of God
you have been chosen to exist.
Here.
Now.
Creation is incomplete without you.
Here.
Now.
You are both wanted and needed.
Here.
Now.
The manner of your entering into existence
is not what defines your being;
the fact that you exist does.
Here.
Now.

To exist means
to have been called into being by love;
to be held in being by love;
to have an ultimate destiny of love.
Here.
Now.
Every experience you have
may be used to teach you
ever-greater depths of love.
Love that transcends desire.
Love that transcends attachment.
Love that transcends self.
Love that prepares you to become love,
so far as you can,
and then enter into
Divine infinite love.
This is the primary vocation
and ultimate destiny of every being.
So begin to live it.
Here.
Now.

Daily Meditation

Breathing in: I have been called into being by love.

Breathing out: I am held by Divine Love.

Repeat this cycle for your meditation practice. If you become distracted, just gently return to the breath without any negative judgement or agitation.

Week Two

Still Point

The Blessing and Challenge of the Present Moment

The constant challenge of the present moment
is
to simply accept it.
Not to dwell
on what it was
or what it should be ...
simply to accept it
as it is.

The constant blessing of the present moment
is that when we accept it
as it is,
we are met
within its beautiful expansiveness
by the mystery
of Divine Love

revealed
in each new moment
as
'I AM' …

This is what the saints
have called
the
sacrament
of the
present moment.

Be still and you will know …

Daily Meditation

Breathing in: I am present in my task.

Breathing out: I am in the presence of God.

Repeat this cycle for your meditation practice. If you become distracted, just gently return to the breath without any negative judgement or agitation.

Week Three

Still Point

Beginning, Always Beginning ...

One of the great gifts of mindfulness practice is its invitation to recognise that we can begin again every day. In the Christian meditative tradition, this constant new beginning is sourced directly from Christ, who as the word of God speaks creation into being, not as a simple historical event but as a constant holding in being through infinite love. This discovery allows us to begin in Christ again, and again, and again ...

As an ancient story from the time of the first monks teaches, a young monk once asked his master, 'Abba, is it true that we can begin again every day?'

The old monk smilingly replied, 'The truly humble of heart begin again every moment!'

Where do you need to begin again in your life?

What are you doing to encourage or to prevent this new beginning?

What would happen if you granted yourself the gift of beginning again in the presence of Divine Love in each moment?

Daily Meditation

Take a moment to become aware of the rhythm of your breath. It is the physical reminder of your constant new beginning. To breathe in with attention is to begin again. To breathe out with gratitude is to allow new beginnings to be born in each moment.

Breathing in: Say with the breath: I begin again in this moment.

Breathing out: Say with the breath: I am grateful for a new beginning.

Repeat this cycle for your meditation practice. If you become distracted, just gently return to the breath without any negative judgement or agitation.

Week Four

Still Point

Never Alone

Every day
there is
so much
strength
and
grace
and
beauty
to be
had
in the
knowledge
that you
are
always
being
prayed for;

that you
are never
outside
the embrace
of
Divine Love
and
compassion;
held there
by those
often
hidden souls
who dedicate
their lives
to
meditation
and prayer …
Trust me;
you are
never
alone …

Daily Meditation

Breathing in: I come home to myself.

Breathing out: I let go of all distractions just for this moment.

Repeat this through your meditation practice. If you become distracted, just gently return to the breath without any negative judgement or agitation.

February

Never forget to 'say grace'. Not just over your meals but over your life. 'Grace' is one of the most ancient names for the Divine life and energy that lives within us and holds us in being. To 'say grace', therefore, is to acknowledge with gratitude the blessing that lies at the heart of whatever we are saying thank you for. Never forget to take a moment to breathe, to give thanks and so to appreciate all you have and all who have given for you … You are, after all, the product of so many ancestors who by their love and work and life have eventually resulted in your coming into this world.

The only way to live truly is with the understanding that all is gift, all is grace. The only response to this realisation is gratitude. To spend every day counting our blessings, giving thanks and making of our whole life a eucharistic offering (the very word 'eucharist' means 'to give thanks' in Greek). This is the way to find the grace in every day and in every moment.

Week One

Still Point

The Loving Generosity of God

This week, take a moment to say grace before meals. Consider all of the work of the earth and of human beings that brought your food to your plate. Remember, behind all of this is the loving generosity of God.

Daily Meditation

Breathing in: I dwell in the awareness of my life as Divine gift.

Breathing out: I give thanks for all that I have received.

Repeat this through your meditation practice. If you become distracted, just gently return to the breath without any negative judgement or agitation.

Saying Grace

To say grace
is to acknowledge
that
everything
is gift.
There is
nothing
that you
have not received
from another;
for
even the elements of your
body
are borrowed
from Mother Earth,
who herself
borrowed them
from the stars,
our elder sisters.
So we behold the beauty
of the cosmos
through eyes
sparkling with
starstuff.
All is gift,
arising from
Divine generosity
and loved
into being;

even this
moment.
How could you not
then
breathe
grace,
before meals
and
after meals
and even
during meals;
sometimes stopping,
even mid-chew,
to smile in awe
at the graced awareness
dawning,
that everything
is Divine gift.

Week Two

Still Point

Litany of St Brigid of Kildare for Her Feast Day

St Brigid, together with St Patrick and St Colmcille, is one of the principal patron saints of Ireland. She was a Celtic princess, named after the Pagan goddess of fire and creativity, who after her baptism chose to dedicate her life to Christ. She became the eldress of a huge monastery of both monks and nuns in Kildare in Ireland and was renowned for the miracles she worked, especially of healing. To this day, she is celebrated in Ireland as a wonderful expression of Celtic Christianity and a powerful and strong woman who fought for the rights of the oppressed and brought peace wherever she went.

A litany is more than a list. It is a series of invocations designed to draw us into the memory and presence of the one we invoke. Each title is a drop of awareness that wears down the hard stone of the door of distraction. For the feast of St Brigid (1 February), here is a litany that may be prayed aloud or in the silence of the heart. Pray it simply and in the rhythm of the breath and with a pause between each invocation, and feel your connection with the feminine patron saint of Ireland.

Daily Meditation

Try reading this litany throughout the week as your meditation practice and allow yourself moments of silence to sit with the words. If you become distracted, just gently return to the breath without any negative judgement or agitation. While you may wish to spend time pondering each of the titles of Brigid in your meditation, you may also like to share it with another in which case either of you may intone the invocations with the other responding as in the brackets.

> Brigid of the hearth and the hare (pray for us)
> Brigid of the spark and the flame
> Brigid of the cloak and the veil
> Brigid of the herb and the stars
> Brigid of the byre and the kine
> Brigid of the ill and the old
> Brigid of the young and the wild
> Brigid of the poor and the voiceless
> Brigid of the oak and the staff
> Brigid of the long nights watching
> Brigid of the sun's slow dawning
> Brigid of the moon's spring rising
> Brigid of the first bloom's flowering
> Brigid of the well's gentle healing

Brigid of the earth's old wisdom
Brigid of the nun's deep chanting
Brigid of the high king of heaven
Brigid of the rush-wovencross
Brigid of the shaven head
Brigid of the lost sword
Brigid of the royal house
Brigid abbess of the dual house of prayer
Brigid eldress of the sanctuary's light
Brigid wise woman of the healing touch
Brigid saint of Ireland
(pray for us)

St Brigid's Eve

This night,
they would hang the cloths
for birthing and healing
over the thorn branches
for her blessing,
that as she walked the land
the Divine dew, twice sanctified
by the dawn and the day both,
might soak them sacred again
and enrich them with this vigil's virtue
for the passing of all pain.
This night,
they would sweep the hearth and house
and bless the barn and the beasts,
settling the kine as queens
in the golden hay of gratitude
for their animal alchemy.
This night,
they would leave out
the old gifts of grace,
the milk and the salt and the bread,
and light the lamp in the window
with love for her,
their princess, passing in peace.
This night,
the stranger that knocked
would be welcomed and warmed,
invited to stretch their feet
before the fire

and offer a story to the circle.
This night,
as the moon rose over the mountains
the old songs were sung,
and the women watched and waited
plaiting the rushes and the reeds
into ancient patterns of power.
This night,
as all surrender to sleep
she walks the land lightly,
breathing blessing,
over barn and beast and babe,
she who fears no dark,
goddess named and God reborn,
by water and fire and blood,
in the three who are one.
This night,
our ancient abbess
and lady of the light,
of Kildare's
oaken cell,
she whose cloak enfolds
the land she loves
comes by.
For this night,
is Brigid's
night.

Week Three

Still Point

Loving Mindfully

It may seem strange that a celibate bishop and martyr of the early church became the patron of romantic love, but St Valentine is that man. However, when we realise he was persecuted and tortured for his willingness to celebrate the marriages of Roman soldiers to their beloved in defiance of the command of the emperor of the time, we begin to understand his association with the trials and tribulations of love. He was martyred on or around the Pagan feast of Lupercalia, a time when it was believed the birds chose their mates and couples were betrothed and thus, in his sacrifice of himself for those he loved, he became forever a symbol of the love that transcends mere romanticism and becomes instead a vision of Divine Love.

Daily Meditation

Breathing in: I receive every instance of real love in my life as a reminder of the love of God.

Breathing out: I ask to become the instrument of that love in the world.

Repeat this cycle through your meditation practice. If you become distracted, just gently return to the breath without any negative judgement or agitation.

St Valentine's Night

Tonight,
as I walk through the heaving city
and see the packed restaurants
selling their over-priced food
(special menus for tonight, of course),
the men self-conscious and hurrying with flowers
(held downwards and losing petals as they go),
the shiny shops bedecked in pink
(hearts, hearts everywhere),
and all about me feel the hopes that are raised
(and the hearts that are dashed),
the dreams of desire made visible
(and so often disappointing us as most desires do
in their dissolving into reality),
I wonder to myself what would you have thought
if, as you sat in your cell awaiting the executioner,
you knew that down through the ages
your name would be used as a token for love?
(Or at least what passes for it betimes.)
Do you walk these streets now
at the invocation of your name,
saint and bishop and martyr too?
(The holy always come when they are called, even in jest,
for in jest, as in tears, there is ever room for grace to move
and conquer.)
Do you smile at the crayoned cards of childhood innocence
or bless the hope in the scribble of the secret admirer?
Do you feel in them the echo of the love in your heart
that drew you, lifelong, to the feet of love itself
to give your heart and soul to one whose heart is pierced

not by cupid's arrow but by spear and nail and thorn
(you who ever ached to be united to him)?
Do you see the same love
in the eyes of the passers-by upon the streets
you saw in the dim-lit pupils of the soldiers
you married in the secret catacombs by night
knowing that love may save not just souls
but even lives when lived aright whether
alone or with another.
You answering not to emperor in love's definitions
but to the love that first kindled love and being
in the one holy breath
and made them two to become one
losing their weakness in the other's strength
as water is lost in wine's appearing.
Perhaps, perhaps, perhaps ...
What I may say is certain though,
that if they knew you truly,
they would, alone or with another,
wake up to love.
And when tomorrow comes
and the pink hearts vanish from the streets
while petals are the playthings of the wind,
they would think of all that fades and all that lasts
and touch the deepest part of love that brings the self
unto its knees and points a path beyond any other
to that place that only saints and children know,
where love is all that is and all that is, is love;
there, at the last, finding in your martyr's heart
the blessing they have always sought
from their Valentine.

Week Four

Still Point

Breathing the Presence

Jesus taught us to see the presence of the Holy Spirit as the origin of the breath of life (*pneuma* in Greek). The Holy Spirit as holy breath is our way into awareness of Divine Presence and how God calls us into this awareness. How often do I truly take 'breathing space', becoming aware of the rhythm of my breath as a sacred gift, a Divine 'yes' to my existence that anchors me in the present moment while connecting me to the great cycles of life all around me. Take a moment now to place your hand on your abdomen and notice deeply the gift of breath. Becoming aware of our breathing allows us to make of our breath a prayer and thus to pray always.

Daily Meditation

Many mystics speak of the opening of the eye of love or of

the heart as a necessary step along the road of contemplative awareness. The gaze of this eye is both internal – keeping attentiveness on the self and the movement of the mind and heart – and external – looking towards the presence of God in the world around us. While the definitive opening of this 'eye' is a matter of grace and gift from God, we may in our meditation begin to cultivate the habits necessary to prepare for its opening.

Breathing in: I gaze within and notice my thoughts and affections.

Breathing out: I direct my inner attention to the presence of God and surrender my inner life to Divine Love.

Repeat this cycle through your meditation practice. If you become distracted, just gently return to the breath without any negative judgement or agitation.

Signs of Love

We are constantly being reminded
that we exist in a cosmos
of meaning and purpose.
The smallest of signs,
the simplest of things,
the tiniest of moments
are all part of a constant chorus that sings out:
'You have come from love;
you are being loved,
and if you yield to my infinite love
then you will discover
your meaning and purpose
is to participate in love for eternity!'
Open the eye of your heart
to see the wonders around you
and you will hear in your soul
their call to awaken
to the one who *is* love!

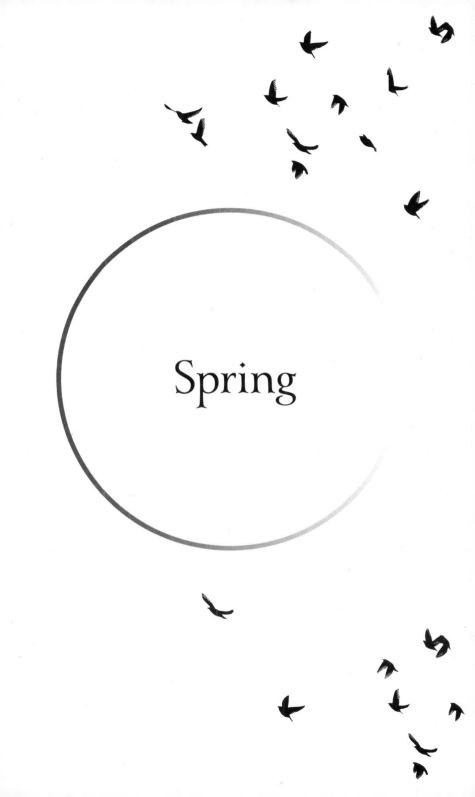

Spring

Getting Out of the Way

We were novices, a word that means 'new'. And we *were* new, new to all of it: new to community life, new to living as brothers, new to the prayers and to the liturgy. Our fingers couldn't yet find the right page in the breviary, the prayer books from which we prayed the psalms together. We were still learning the geography of the friary and its gardens; still learning which of the brothers did what and how to speak to them about it.

We were new to the robe and new to the sandals, all clumsy thumbs and cold toes. Every day, we joined the professed community for meditation; two periods of half an hour before lauds (morning prayer) and vespers (evening prayer). These are the two periods of stillness that, as we were to learn, are the ancient hinges on which, to this day, swing the door of monastic, meditative prayer, the door that slowly opens you to the presence of the one who *is*.

But we were novices. I myself was barely 19, definitely new, and so those periods were spent trying to resist distraction – trying not to look at the clock, trying not to fall asleep or, if I did fall asleep, trying to do so in such a way that the novice master wouldn't notice! Sometimes, those periods were even spent keeping one eye open and scanning the faces of the older brothers who seemed, effortlessly, to sink into a profound silence and stillness that had a quality of presence and peace to it that we as yet could barely fathom.

We soon recognised that among the brethren there was one brother whose silence spoke to us novices louder than any of the books on meditation we had been given. He would enter the choir (the wood-panelled private chapel of the friary) with the rest of the brothers, make his genuflection towards the blessed sacrament and then he would simply ... sit. His body folding into prayer with the ease of a well-oiled mechanism seemed so used to these movements from countless repetitions. He sat a little forward, his spine straight, his eyes closed, his hands deftly folded in his lap, his breathing so deep that it was barely perceptible. He was alert and relaxed, peaceful and dynamic, still and yet vibrating with energy. His name was Brother Berard; and he was, we novices agreed among ourselves, the best at all this ... and probably a saint to boot.

So you can imagine our excitement when a few weeks later, our novice master told us that we would be taking lessons in meditation with Brother Berard. We talked about what we would ask him, mentally got our questions ready and spent quite a few meditation periods surreptitiously studying him closely.

Finally, the morning came.

We gathered around the table in the novitiate classroom.

He came in quietly, said a short prayer invoking the Holy Spirit, Our Lady and St Francis, as was always the custom before a talk, and then he sat with us. We were silent. He glanced at us with bright eyes that belied his age, steepled his hands, looked at the ground and, in his slow, deep voice asked us what we understood by the word 'meditation'.

It was as though a dam had burst! Questions, comments, theories tumbled out of us born of our few weeks of frustrated, distracted 'practice'. When, at last, we were done, Brother Berard, who had not moved throughout, regarded us for a moment in silence and gently said, 'Sons, meditation is simply closing your eyes and getting out of God's way.'

We were stunned, we had expected techniques, secrets, teachings … It was to be a few months before we were to realise that, in that one single sentence, we had received all of that and more besides.

As the weeks went on, Brother Berard did teach us deeply; we encountered our minds and their multiple layers, we dwelt in our breath, learned to recognise both distractions and the touches of grace that came in their midst and often despite them, and we were taught not to get attached to either, letting each simply arise, be and depart. We learned the ancient techniques for centring our attention, becoming mindful, stilling the thoughts, and becoming present to the one who *is* always present to us in love. We were slowly learning to get out of God's way … something I am still learning to do to this day.

What sounded simple on that winter's morning in the novitiate seems now to be the work of a lifetime, and the discipline that truly allows us to be a real disciple is one that must be embraced daily and even begun again in every moment.

Now that I find myself teaching others the way of mindfulness, the way of meditative prayer in the Christian tradition, I hear myself quoting Brother Berard often. His words and, above all, the example of his practice still invite me to deepen my own stillness, mindfulness and presence so as to encounter Divine Presence. To meet the one who is waiting to be met and who abides at our centre in our inner room.

Let's try then, each day and even in each moment, to get out of God's way.

Meeting Otherness

When you meet the other,
whoever they are,
stop.
Just stop.
Stop
long enough
to become
present
to their
being
as a door
to
Divine Presence …
When you meet the other,
whoever they are,
bow.
Just bow.
Bow
low enough
to reverence
their being
as a gift
held in existence
by
Divine Love …
When you meet the other,
whoever they are,
listen.
Just listen.

Listen
long enough
to hear
their truth
revealed
as a page
of the story
written by
the
Divine word …
When you meet the other,
whoever they are,
stop.
Just stop.
Bow.
Just bow.
Listen.
Just listen.
And then,
only then,
in the
hallowed
space
between you
and the other,
whoever they are,
speak.

March

Mindful Mornings

An old priest once said to me that there are two ways to begin every day.

'We can say, "Good God, it's morning!" Or we can say, "Good morning, God!"

Our first thoughts shape our day, so let them be compassionate, gentle, mindful and prayerful, and we will see the results as the day unfolds.

Try thinking about how you usually begin your day. Is it filled with worry, stress or seeking news of the world out there? Or is it gentle, nourishing, prayerful, calm and loving to those around you?

Reinvigorate the old practice of the morning offering. The monastic tradition has always seen the first moment of the day as a special time of grace in which we can connect with the Divine Presence and enter the day prayerfully, mindful of our relationship with God and with all creation. Make it your habit to spend the first moment of the day in conscious awareness of Divine Love, offering all that will come up during the day so as to live immersed in Divine Love and blessing.

A physical gesture, such as a slow signing of the cross, a genuflection or bow, or kneeling as you pray, can often make this moment much more significant and memorable, so that a sense of offering may accompany you through the day.

March Moon

To walk the edge
of between,
by
the light of the
rising
full
yellow moon
of
March,
bestows the bright
blessing
of the
hare,
who leaps
heavenwards
joining
sky and sea
in a moment
of shining stillness.
Breathe deeply
of the
spring-scented dark
and
watch, as
the
branches,
rocks,
waves,
sands

hear the sacred
summons
and all appear anew
from the
dark of dusk
where they had
been
hiding in
shapeless
shadow,
like children
beneath their
blankets
feigning sleep
until,
woken by her
rose-gold grace,
they
dress themselves
anew in
light,
and dance
until day
to the song
of the
stars.

Week One

Still Point

Holy Readiness

Holy Readiness
is
the art of
attuned awareness;
having in itself
both
stillness and activity.
Poised listening
in the between,
it opens up
to the infinitude
of Divine spaciousness
as choice.
Originating from
restfulness
it flies from tension
and simply
abides

in reflective
quiet,
until
aspiration
becomes
inspiration,
and
action flows
with
grace,
advancing
Divine purpose
through
compassion,
as the
bell of the heart
sounds
the note
of
truth
and
love,
and brings,
always,
blessing.

Daily Meditation

Breathing in: I begin my day in awareness of Divine Presence.

Breathing out: I offer all I am to become the instrument of Divine Love.

Repeat this cycle during your meditation practice. If you become distracted, just gently return to the breath without any negative judgement or agitation.

Week Two

Still Point

Never a Room

There is never
a room
that you will enter
that Divine Love
is not
already
within.
There is never
a conversation
that you will have
that Divine silence
is not already
a part of.
There is never
a place that you will go to
that Divine providence
is not
already

holding in being.
There is never
a person you will meet
who is not
already
the temple of Divine Presence.
There is never
a wound suffered
that is not
already
an encounter with Divine mercy.
There is never
a breath you will breathe
that is not
already
the Divine breath breathing
in your breath
the breath of love.
There is never
a moment you will pass
that is not
already
an experience of the Divine now of grace.
So be at peace.
Then
simply and gently
yield
to the awareness of
Divine Presence,
and know
that in the yielding

is the
awareness
of
love.

Daily Meditation

Breathing in: I will return to awareness of Divine Presence often.

Breathing out: I offer my gratitude for the gift of this precious life.

Repeat this cycle during your meditation practice. If you become distracted, just gently return to the breath without any negative judgement or agitation.

Week Three

Still Point

The feast of St Joseph is on 19 March. Like Abraham, Moses and even Mary, Joseph did not know his destiny as he lived his life. But, like them, he chose to live in the presence of God in each moment and thus was able to hear the word of God when it was addressed to him in his dreams and to live in faithful obedience to the call of God.

In meditating on the life of Joseph, often called the 'universal patron', we can learn many lessons for your meditative life. Here are some of them:

We have no idea what God is planning for us; only that it is always for our good. God does not pre-emptively remove doubt or fear or suffering; rather, he asks us to surrender them to him and simply follow his way in love, thus transforming them into tools for spiritual growth.

We can make mistakes thinking that we are doing the good or even the will of God, but angels will always be sent to invite us back to the way. Our job is to ensure that we do not allow the despair or guilt we may feel over our mistakes and sins to drown out the angelic voices or blind us to their presence, however hidden they may be in their appearance.

God uses the most ordinary of our human circumstances – our family, our community, our travels and our daily work – to reveal the deepest significance of our being as beloved children of God.

God reveals himself far more clearly in our rest, in our stillness, in our peaceful sleep and in our silence than He does in our activity or our words.

Mastery, whether spiritual or work-based, is a matter of discipline, repetition and heart – not words, publicity or show.

Only by becoming what we are in the mind of God do we touch true peace. Prayer, meditation and contemplation is the path and the instrument of this becoming. Our job is simply to be faithful to the present moment and to its ever-new invitation to choose the way of light, to do the Divine will.

Daily Meditation

Praying with our dreams

Try and think of a time when your dreams seemed to offer guidance or even nearness to the presence of God. These don't just have to be the dreams we receive as we sleep; even our waking 'day-dreams' can reveal much about how we think and what we give our inner attention to. Take a little time this week to pay attention to your dreams.

Breathing in: I give thanks for the presence of sleep and dreams in my life.

Breathing out: I ask that God's dream for me and for the world moves forward.

Repeat this cycle during your meditation practice. If you become distracted, just gently return to the breath without any negative judgement or agitation.

Week Four

Still Point

Coming Home to Yourself

At a time when we live very distracted lives and are often on the go, it can be difficult to make time for prayer, for peace, for mindful awareness of God. But if we slow down and breathe gently and prayerfully, then we will find that God is always waiting for us at the deepest point of our being. We can come home to our self in God by following the path of breath.

Sit in stillness. Rest in your breath, close your eyes to distraction, allow your mind to dwell in your heart, your inner space of love where Divine Love always is. And then you will slowly begin to perceive the gentle movement and call of the heavenly dove whose inner light will penetrate your darkness, whose song will call you home to yourself, home to the embrace of Divine Love. Be still … and you will know …

Daily Meditation

Breathing In: I come home to myself.

Breathing Out: I let go of all distractions just for this moment.

Repeat this cycle during your meditation practice. If you become distracted, just gently return to the breath without any negative judgement or agitation.

April

* Some thoughts for the Easter season are in a special section, 'From Lent to Easter' on page 317.

Dealing with the Distractions: The Meditation Gym

There is a wonderful story from the life of that great mystic and master of meditation, St Teresa of Ávila, that deals with distractions in prayer beautifully.

Having been brought to a convent of sisters to teach them about the way of meditation, she did so in great depth and with much skill. However, towards the end of her time with them, she was asked by one of the sisters to describe how she herself meditated.

Taking the last half hour that the sisters had gathered, she began by saying she had gone to the chapel with them, genuflected before the Lord in the blessed sacrament and interiorly dedicated the time of prayer to him. Then she'd sat in stillness – and almost immediately was distracted!

But she remembered she was there to pray and returned to her meditation ... and was immediately distracted again. But she remembered she was there to pray and returned to her meditation ...

St Teresa continued to describe the ongoing oscillation from distraction to distraction that, to her listeners, seemed to comprise the whole of her meditation, much to the dismay of the sisters who wanted to learn from this master of prayer.

At the end, one of them was so amazed she blurted out, 'But then you were just distracted for the whole of your meditation!'

'Ah,' said Teresa, smiling, 'yes, I was distracted, but I returned each time. And that makes all the difference.'

Perhaps one of the most common difficulties in prayer that is brought to me both as a teacher and as a confessor is the whole area of distractions during meditation.

People can often torture themselves over this perceived difficulty; indeed, for some, the encounter with the dross and ephemera that arises before their mind's eye during meditation can be so off-putting and the struggle to defeat them so exhausting that it puts them off the practice of meditation completely.

So let's look at the general problem of distractions and how we should deal with them in meditation.

You see, the problem often begins with dividing our assessment of our period of meditation into 'the time I was distracted', which often seems like the majority of our time, and 'the time I was meditating', which usually seems like the minority, when the real issue is that we are approaching the meditation from the wrong perspective by using this as the framework of our division of the time in the first place.

The problem is further compounded when we add a layer of guilt and self-recrimination for the distractions. This, in turn, arouses anxiety and further separates us from the relaxed stillness necessary to our prayer. These difficulties arise when we fail to realise that the distractions are a part, indeed a very necessary part, of the meditative process. I will repeat that: The distractions are part of the discipline of prayer.

Let me explain ...

Suppose as part of your fitness plan, you decided you wanted to build up your biceps. You go to the gym and, with effort, you lift a weight. (So far so good.) But then you *never* put it down again. Do you build the muscle? No, of course not; in fact you will probably wither it and end up with less movement and less muscle. It is in both the contraction and the release, the picking up of the weight and the putting it down again, that the strength of the muscle is built when the process is repeated over and over again. The same is true for the mind at prayer.

Every time a distraction arises, and we notice we are distracted, we simply and gently return to the anchors of the breath and the prayer word that draws us back to our focused mindful awareness of the Divine Presence. The taking up of the time of prayer is the picking up of the weight. The distraction arising is the releasing of the weight. As long as we pick up the weight again as soon as we notice that we have put it down, we are building the 'muscle' of the attention, refining our mindful awareness a little more each time, so that over the days, weeks, months and years of practice, the distractions become less and the periods between them become longer. Indeed, after a time the distractions will simply rise and fall but our own focus on the presence will remain true beneath and beyond them.

This 'discipline of distraction' is actually essential to the beginner in meditative prayer and is the whole of the art in its initial stages. It refines focus, builds attention in a gentle way, opens the present moment as the place of encounter with the Divine Presence, and deepens our humility and the awareness of our need for Divine grace.

In coming back again and again and again, we are allowing the Holy Spirit to write the path of *metanoia*, the path of conversion (literally re-turning to God) within our hearts. It is on and in this struggle *(ascesis)* for mindful attention that the desert fathers and mothers saw the foundations of the real meditative life being built, and it was the art that the monastic had to be grounded in before moving on to deeper forms of meditative prayer.

As the great master of prayer St Francis de Sales wrote in his wonderful treatise *Introduction to the Devout Life*:

> If the heart wanders or is distracted, bring it back to the point quite gently and replace it tenderly in its master's presence. And even if you did nothing during the whole hour [of meditation] but bring your heart back and place it in Our Lord's presence, though it went away every time you brought it back, your hour would be very well employed.

So then, the next time you go to sit, and you notice the distractions arise … smile. And then immediately return to the breath and begin again … and again … and again. This is the discipline of meditation, this is the path of prayer, this is the way to build mindful attention of the Divine Presence. And as you leave your meditation, if anyone asks you what you were doing in there just say, 'Working out!'

Week One

Still Point

The Mindful Discipline of Lent

All of our Lenten discipline – our prayer, our fasting, our almsgiving (charitable action for others) – amounts simply to this: to allow the pure water of grace cleanse the eye of awareness of all distraction from Divine Light; to allow the embrace of holy desire awaken our hearts to Divine Love; to allow the healing breath of the Holy Spirit vivify in us Divine life. For when we allow this Divine activity, we become the place where the bearing of the cross becomes the place of resurrection for us and for all. In this, we see that the events of Holy Week and Easter are not just something that took place a long time ago but are an eternal event that may be enacted in and through the person who opens themselves to the redeeming grace of Christ offered to all from moment to moment as a new beginning in love.

Ask yourself: 'How will I live this Lenten season in a more mindful, aware way? What will I take on or give up to make more space for meditation and prayer? How does my prayer affect the way I treat others?'

Daily Meditation

Breathing in: I invoke the Holy Spirit to awaken my heart to Divine Love.

Breathing out: I choose to be an instrument of healing and peace in the world.

Repeat this cycle during your meditation practice. If you become distracted, just gently return to the breath without any negative judgement or agitation.

Week Two

Still Point

Mindful Work is Working for the Kingdom

There is no job so seemingly small or humble that will not build the kingdom of God's love and compassion when it is done with the heart, with mindful awareness and with the right intention.

This is meditation in action.

This is the contemplative way.

From our sitting in meditation, we are changed and healed.

By working meditatively, we co-operate with God in the healing of the cosmos.

The smallest act of kindness, of love or of faithful duty has eternal significance when we invite the Divine Presence to breathe through it and fill it with love.

This week, bring the awareness of your breath to mind when you go about your daily tasks. Spend a moment before work in prayer and dedicate the time and the work to the building of the kingdom of God in the world. Nothing, not even taking out the rubbish, is a waste of time when we bring attention and prayer to the work at hand.

Daily Meditation

Breathing in: I will work in each moment aware of God's presence.

Breathing out: I breathe out peace.

Repeat this cycle during your meditation practice. If you become distracted, just gently return to the breath without any negative judgement or agitation.

Desert Stillness

Be still
and know
that I am ...
Would you enter the desert
at the heart of yourself?
Would you allow the sandals of your senses
to fall away?
Would you, finally, recognise
the holy ground your heart
truly is?
Would you behold the burning bush
afire with presence at the centre of
your soul?
Then you must
enter the desert of stillness.
Be still
and know ...
Would you know the call to exodus
from the slavery of self?
Would you pass through the waters
of overwhelming worry?
Would you ascend the holy mountain of prayer?
Would you behold the glory so bright that it is darkness?
Would you enter the cloud of the presence?
Would you keep the covenant of grace?
Would you reach the promised land of peace?
Then you must enter the desert of stillness.
Be still
and know ...
For

this is how the ultimate is revealed:
as presence through stillness,
as being beyond being,
as emptiness without absence,
as right relationship,
in which
we come to know
the self truly
only in the light
of pure being as
independent
(where all else depends on love),
as non-contingent
(where all else arises from previous causes),
as creative
(where all else sub-creates),
as transcending all,
imminent in all,
beyond all,
but
holding all
in being
by
love.
Would you enter the desert
at the heart of yourself
and see it bloom?
If you would,
then only
be still
and you will
know.

STILL POINTS

Week Three

Still Point

The Reason for It All

In the end, we realise that everything that is comes from infinite, unconditional Divine Love.

We come from that love and are on a path of return to it.

You do not need to frantically seek love, to possess love, to control love.

You are already loved just by being you.

You just need to realise that every instance of love you experience in this life is simply meant to be a reminder of the infinite love that already holds you in being.

Breathe deep.

Rest in that love today.

When anxiety calls, remember that the foundation of your very existence is love.

Anxiety, worry, stress … these things will come and go and come again.

Beneath them all, behind them all, is the simple truth: you are loved.

So many of the saints teach us, over and over again, that the primary reason for the incarnation of the word, for the life, death, resurrection and ascension of Jesus, was simply this: to prove to you just how much you are loved.

Daily Meditation

Breathing in: I rest in the infinite and unconditional love of God for me.

Breathing out: I let go of all needless anxiety and worry.

Repeat this cycle during your meditation practice. If you become distracted, just gently return to the breath without any negative judgement or agitation.

Week Four

Still Point

Easter is a New Beginning in Every Moment

The gift of Easter is that no matter what has happened to us, our past is not meant to be a place to dwell in regret or guilt, but a place where only mercy and love is known that allows it to become a store of wisdom that we draw on to deepen the present and inform the future.

The gift of Easter means that no matter how worried or anxious we are, the future is not meant to be anything other than a blank page wherein each moment we co-operate with Divine providence in writing the story of love, a story that has been unfolding since the first moment of creation and which will continue for eternity.

The gift of Easter means that no matter how distracted we are, or unable to see it, the present is not meant to be anything other than holy; sacred ground on which we learn that if we simply slow down and breathe deeply, then every leaf of every bush is aflame with the glory of God and every moment is a revelation of Divine Presence holding all things in being through love.

Sacred Pause

How will I live the light of Easter each day? What in me must be brought to the light of Easter so as to begin again?

Daily Meditation

Breathing in: I give thanks for this new beginning.

Breathing out: I choose to begin again in every moment.

Repeat this cycle during your meditation practice. If you become distracted, just gently return to the breath without any negative judgement or agitation.

Crocus

Once, long ago,
during a winter more grey within
than cold without,
when the house was filled
with seeming endless
sadness, and anger,
and emptiness,
I came down one morning
to a chilled and silent kitchen
to discover that outside,
a crocus had bloomed overnight,
under the old cherry tree,
in a place none had ever bloomed before.
How had it come there on that day,
in that place?
Bird-carried, wind-blown
or old planting stirred anew?
But, why wonder at its coming?
All it asked of me
was to be seen.
I stood, still,
empty kettle in hand,
staring into the grey garden,
now sunlit, with the yellow frail petals
of an unexpected
and unlooked-for flower.
It lasted just long enough
for us to hear,
behind the song of sorrow

we were singing in that house then,
a note of hope, a sound of spring,
not now, but coming.
I knew then, and for evermore,
that at the right time, in the right place,
looked at in the right way,
even a tiny yellow crocus
can be a word from the Word.
So today I know that
when sadness sings her song
around my roots,
it is okay,
it is beautiful,
it is necessary,
but also it is an invitation
to wait and watch
for the yellow crocus
to bloom again,
as it always will,
announcing angel-like
the nearness of spirit's spring,
not now, perhaps,
but always coming.

May

Traditionally, the month of May is dedicated to Mary, the mother of God. For the contemplative Christian, Mary is the great example and guide along the path of prayer.

She is the one human being who is perfectly united to the holy trinity: as daughter of the Father, mother of the Son and spouse of the Holy Spirit. It is through the 'yes' of Mary that we receive every Divine gift and grace. She is the perfect example of one who abides always in the presence of God and who from that abiding awareness draws the strength to live a constant 'yes' to the Divine will.

As May issues in the full flowering of the year, it reminds us that our full flowering and fruiting as human beings depend on our living in the presence of Divine Love. Mary shows us the way and walks our journey with us, inviting us to live in the presence of God with full awareness in each moment, just as she did.

The Rosary: A Mindful Walk with Mary

The Holy Rosary is not merely a bland ritual or old devotion but a profoundly deep school of contemplative prayer that, when practised properly, slowly draws one from the very beginnings of petitionary prayer to the prayer of quiet and thence to the prayer of union. The Rosary is an ancient beloved form of meditation on the life of Jesus and Mary prayed through the repetition of the Hail Mary, often while using beads to deepen the meditation.

While often beginning as a devotional practice in its early stages of use, the Rosary can bring us to the heights of wordless prayer that seeks only to abide in Divine Presence and love as it speaks to every aspect of our being. Drawing us into stillness of the body and mind through the repetitive passing of the beads through the fingers, it cultivates the faculty of the imagination, drawing the rational mind into a deep *lectio* or spiritual reading of the Divine mysteries of the life of Jesus and the blessed mother (especially when combined with the reading of sacred scripture relating to these mysteries), and so arouses in the heart-centre a readiness for the gifts of true compunction and compassion that mark the work of the purifying power of the Holy Spirit to bring about the deepest conversion of heart ... or perfect *metanoia*.

Going beyond this stage, the praying of the Rosary can become the way to arrive at the fulfilment of that desire of Christ that we would pray always (it is in fact the Western version of the Jesus Prayer, having at its heart the prayerful repetition of the holy name at the centre of every Hail Mary), and through the mindful repetition of the prayer in its turning cycle, we arrive at the beginnings of that resting in the Divine Presence that marks the prayer of quiet and the beginning of the apophatic path to the true prayer of union.

The extraordinary value of this holy practice as a school

of prayer and sanctity is borne out by the countless saints, doctors, popes and holy men and women of every age who have recommended it as the quickest and surest way to walk with Christ in deep prayer through inviting Mary his mother (from whom all that was human in Christ is received, and through whom all that is Divine in Christ is received), to guide us in the way of perfect union with the holy trinity – a unity which she herself never lost.

So what are you waiting for? I have a short section at the end of this book on The Rosary, so turn to page 344 and take up your beads ...

Rosary

Unite
bead with
breath
and being,
so that
awareness
appears.
Inspiration
ignites
love's
luminescence
as
mysteries
manifest
in
meditation
with
the
mother
and
then,
in heat of
heart's
hearth,
warmed by
wonder,
the seed of
silence
long planted

in
prayerful
possibility
grows
greatly
until,
in
sacred
stillness,
the
red rose
buds,
and
blooms,
blessing.

Week One

Still Point

Nature as Teacher

Nature is a wonderful teacher of the mindful, contemplative life.

The bad weather allows us to rejoice even more in the good – without the storms we would never see the rainbow.

A beautiful rainbow lasts for five minutes and then fades away … it will never come again in the same exact way and this gives me two choices: to be sad that it's gone and to cling to the experience or to rejoice that I saw it at all and to let it go. If I choose the latter, then I simply honour the rainbow as gift, I become open to the lesson it teaches and to the next experience of the present moment.

Whatever you are going through today, remember you are going *through* it. No experience or emotional state is everlasting in this life.

Joys and sorrows arise and then depart until they come again.

You are not your feelings and you are not defined by them, unless you cling to them.

Breath by breath, moment by moment, we learn that, in fact, we are travelling through this experience towards becoming our real self, revealed in the light of love as being and not simply just as feeling.

For life is a journey into the mystery of Divine Love.

Into the mystery of God who *is* love.

Daily Meditation

Breathing in: I become aware of my feelings.

Breathing out: I allow my feelings to come and go.

Repeat this cycle during your meditation practice. If you become distracted, just gently return to the breath without any negative judgement or agitation.

Week Two

Still Point

Contemplation

*Contemplation is the entering of a silence
impregnated with Divine Love.*

St Gregory the Great

Come to the silence in yourself,
the deep silence that exists
behind the noise and before the sound.
Come to the Word
who is silent love
who is eternity itself
who is the thunder in the void.
Come to the one
who holds you in being
now, in this moment, in love.
Come to the one
who proves this love
by emptying himself into time
until, in utter vulnerability,

he becomes food;
filling our hungry silence
with love.

Daily Meditation

Breathing in: I come home to myself.

Breathing out: I let go of all distractions just for this moment.

Repeat this cycle during your meditation practice. If you become distracted, just gently return to the breath without any negative judgement or agitation.

Week Three

Still Point

The Child and the Saint

The gift of the child and the gift of the saint are one and the same; it is the gift of entering their inner silence, the place where imagination is sanctified by grace, so well that they can hear the voices by which everything is talking They know that everything is inviting you into the dance of Divine Love if you just listen deeply enough.

The innocence of the child allows them to enter the world of imagination and there become aware that everything is speaking in its own language. The innocence of the saint, won back by prayer and meditation, allows them to hear not just the inner voices of creation but the voice of God speaking through creation.

The child and the saint are seen to dance to music that no one else can hear; in their imagining they allow the gift of the spirit to whisper its song of wonder and wisdom and wildness. They feel deeply and know that they may become the best possible person in each moment. Every morning is a new beginning and the world is fresh and beautiful.

So what of us? Can we follow the path of the child, becoming childlike again, as Christ himself has commanded for those who would enter the kingdom of heaven? If then, you simply slow down, dwell in the simple joys of life and nature, let go of the noise of your thoughts, become quiet and breathe deep, you will rediscover the voices of the cosmos that will invite you to hear the Divine voice behind all things, and play.

Daily Meditation

Breathing in: I invite the Holy Spirit to restore the gift of wonder and awe in me.

Breathing out: I look out on the world with love.

Repeat this cycle during your meditation practice. If you become distracted, just gently return to the breath without any negative judgement or agitation.

Week Four

Still Point

Purposeful Presence Pause

Let your daily journey
be punctuated with
pauses of presence,
by which you become present
to Divine Love.
For Divine Love
is always present to you!
Become still.
Breathe deep.
Look at the beauty
around you,
and within you.
Give thanks!
This is a purposeful presence pause.

Daily Meditation

Breathing in: I rest in the Divine Presence within.

Breathing out: I breathe peace to all around me.

Repeat this cycle during your meditation practice. If you become distracted, just gently return to the breath without any negative judgement or agitation.

Let the Moon of Meditation Rise

Our Lady is the moon
who reflects perfectly the light of the
sun who is the Son.
Mary teaches us the way of contemplation,
the way of becoming so still
that the light of the Lord
rises in our souls and shines out
from our hearts
then drawing others to his infinite love.
Become still,
breathe deep,
look within
and watch the moon of meditation
rise.

Summer

Of Weedkiller and Wonder

I'm ashamed to say it, but it all began with weedkiller. And looking back now, the fact that I even thought of weedkiller as a solution to the problem is a source of horror and embarrassment. Or perhaps it began with the feeling of frustration at needing to ask for it ...

As novices, one of the duties we had was to assist the brother who looked after the extensive novitiate gardens. He was an elderly brother, a gentle confessor to the people who sought him out in the church, but he was most at home in the silence of the gardens where he kept us supplied with fresh vegetables and, in the autumn, sweet apples and pears. These were traditional cloister gardens that only the novices and the novitiate staff used. As a young novice of 19, I loved them. There were beautiful old fruit trees, vegetable patches, an extraordinary spliced laburnum tree that flowered spectacularly once a year in a half-yellow and half-purple explosion, lots of small green lawns and fulsome flowerbeds, and, around them all and through them all, long gravel paths that led to little shrines and hidden areas set aside for prayer, reflection, reading or simply enjoying the autumnal sunshine in those first months of the ancient yearlong retreat experience we call novitiate.

Working with the brother gardener meant mowing lawns and trimming trees and planting and hoeing and doing all the usual jobs that a large garden needs while learning the arcane arts of gardening. We three novices worked in a rotation: one on fruit and veg, one on lawns and flowers, and one on the dreaded weeding of the paths.

Then came the day the rotation shifted and suddenly I found myself moved on to path-weeding duty. Three times a week I would spend an afternoon kneeling on the path plucking out the little sprouts of dandelions, daisies and other invaders that threatened to overcome the order of the paths and bind the gravel together into a muddy mess. Having completed the section I was working on, I would then hoe and rake the gravel back into order before the bell rang for evening meditation and prayer.

Looking back as I left, I would notice that the section I had just worked on was clean and clear, but whatever satisfaction I was taking in my work for that day would be miserably mitigated by seeing the apparent miles that awaited my attention in front of me, to say nothing of the light green fuzz already accruing on the section I had done the previous week. I hated it.

To my mind it was back-breaking and slow and stupid. I could not understand why so much time was being expended on maintaining the paths by hand when surely a once-a-month treatment with weedkiller would have rendered them just as free for much longer and would have freed me in the process for much more necessary and important work.

And so I would spend my time, kneeling on the paths no longer focused on the beauty of the gardens but grumbling deep within – especially when other friars passed me by mowing grass, digging beds and generally seeming to have a much better time than I was.

Then came a particularly bad day. It had rained the day before. The path was muddy. The roots were deep. My back was sore. All through evening meditation, I ached and fulminated in equal quantities as, around me, the gentle breathing of the brethren did nothing to calm my mood. Tomorrow, I resolved, I would do something about it – and so I did.

As soon as the morning classes were over, I asked to see the novice master. Sitting in front of him, I made my request for money to go and get weed-killer for the paths. I was reasonable in my tone, clear in my arguments. I enunciated my request calmly, being sure to stress that this would make the job easier not just for me but for everyone.

'Think of all the time that would be saved,' I said.

'I'm surprised no one has ever thought of this before,' I said.

'I'll be free to do so much more,' I said.

The novice master just looked at me.

Then, when I had quite finished and talked myself into silence, he said quietly, 'Brother, when you can come to me and tell me why I'm refusing your request now, then you won't have to weed the paths any more.'

There was a moment of silence and then, stunned slightly, I left the room.

Over the ensuing days and weeks, I grew to dread those paths. And always, as I was working, I would stew over what the novice master had said. Was it because we never used chemicals in the garden elsewhere? Was it a Franciscan thing? Was he just being cheap? Was it supposed to be penance? (It certainly felt like it at times.) And so I grumbled and weeded and made my way slowly around the paths for about a month, feeling the encroaching green army always at my sandalled heels and losing no opportunity to tell the brothers what I thought of weedkiller and weeds and futile work until I'm sure they longed for the bell to ring that ushered in silent time in the evenings.

Then, one day, out of the blue, and a day in all respects like any other, it happened. I was weeding away. In the background, I could hear the other brothers chatting as they worked on the fruit trees. It was a sunny, brisk day and I could feel the earth drying on my fingers as I parted another weed from the ground and pulled it free from the gravel. And then, just as I shook it, watching the clods of mud fall away from the roots, something fell away from me as surely as the grains of soil fell to the ground. I can only say I was freed, that I was connected.

Connected to the gravel.

Connected to the root.

Connected to the earth beneath.

Connected to the sunshine.

Connected to the dust.

Connected to the breath.

Connected to the love that holds it all in being.

I was myself apart and I was connected to all of it.

It did not matter that I was weeding or not weeding.

It did not matter that the paths were greening behind me and were still green before me.

There was just me in this moment.

Now.

Performing this action.

Now.

Breathing and moving.

Now.

Loving and being loved.

Now.

I kept on weeding, but it was as though a deep quality of experience that is always just below the surface had been revealed. I realised that we float on the surface of a deep ocean of being. It was like seeing a familiar but dark room illuminated dazzlingly as a curtain is suddenly pulled back. Everything was still in the room, all the familiar furniture was there but brightened and outlined in sunshine.

It wasn't peaceful, it was peace.

It wasn't joyful, it was joy.

It wasn't loving, it was love.

It wasn't praying, it was prayer.

And I ... well, I kept weeding! What else could you do?

It only lasted a moment, though it seemed to expand within me and around me forever, and then (foolishly, I know now) I looked at it, not from within but from without and began to rejoice not *in* the experience but at *having* the experience and, as my ego awoke, immediately it vanished.

At first I was sad, but then I smiled and kept on weeding. After all, that was the job in hand.

From then on, weeding was no longer the burden it had been. It was just weeding. It didn't matter that I would be kneeling in an island of soon-to-be-consumed-again grey, loose gravel. There was just this moment, this weed, this job, this breath ... and that was okay.

The rhythm of weeding – of bending, bowing, plucking, shaking, hoeing, raking – became the background music to an inner attention to the prayer of the breath that today, many years of practice later, I know marked the beginning of the mindfulness of Divine Presence that is the foundation stone of Christian meditation practice. Over the weeks I grew to quite like weeding; all thoughts of weedkiller were forgotten. I simply dwelt in the ordinary wonder of the garden.

Later, I discussed the experience with the novice master. He smiled, said nothing about it then but, the following day, he relieved me of weeding duty.

Over the months, the experience would come and go. I realised it could never be forced, though it could be encouraged and it always happened when I was just in the moment, in a fluidity of being that very often brought body and mind together in a repetitive, disciplined action, in which intention had been set to dwell fully in the work and be fully present to it, while preserving a loving attention at the centre of the heart on the Divine Presence. There is a reason we call it cultivation – this work of attuning the inner attention to that which is always present to us. It takes a lifetime to master but the joy is in knowing that when we begin to practise, Divine Love swoops down into the gap between what we are (our usual distracted, self-centred existence) and what we could be (centred, peaceful, present) and gives us a glimpse of the latter so that we might wish to work on the former.

If you would like to begin to weed out your own distractions, so as to begin to enter this mindfulness of presence, then a few suggestions come from the tradition.

Intentionality
Consciously make a prayer, setting your intention to be present to Divine Love every day. If possible, do this first thing in the morning (the morning-offering practice). It can be good to return to this prayer at midday and in the evening. Invite the Holy Spirit to begin the work of attuning you to his presence and inspiration.

Sitting
Simply begin by setting two periods of about 20 minutes, morning and evening, to sit comfortably but alertly. If 20 minutes is too long, start with 10 and allow it to grow. Invoke the Holy Spirit and offer the time to the Lord as a time of being consciously present to him by being consciously present to the reality of his love breathing through you, and then follow the gentle rhythm of your breath as it rises and falls. You may add a prayer word to this later, but, for now, just follow the breath and, when you become distracted, return to it gently and without stress.

Work
We are all busy people, but our work, whatever it is, can still be prayer. Moving from activity to activity, pause long enough to reset your intention each time to be inwardly present to the Divine Presence within and around you. A simple moment in which you breathe deeply, three rounds of in-breath and out-breath, dedicating each one to the

Father, the Son and the Holy Spirit can be a beautiful way to do this. In time, you will need to reset less and less.

Finally
Please don't use weedkiller!

June

With the coming of June, we enter the season in all its raucous colour as we move from the pale sun of its earliest days to the high heat of midsummer. It is a time to appreciate beauty, to stop and look around, to rest and be renewed.

Early Summer Vespers at Ards Friary

The hour of vespers arrives,
as the bell of the heart
tolls its sunset tone
at the decline of the day,
and gentles the soul
with the lapping of waves
and the curlew's cry.
The earth exhales,
surrendering her warmth
to the dusking sky
as gift, in that ancient choral
rhythm of interbeing,
bridged by greened canopy
of summer leaves.
Heaven hushes, and
liberates the busy
into pools of pausing
and introspection which,
for a moment, invite stillness
and, perhaps, praise.
Blessing falls on all
with sunset's revelation
of the first star,
whose purpled light
draws towards rest,
and sleep, and dream;
while always Francis
keeps his vigil,

and, as herald of Divine
new beginning,
watches for the first
bird's song of night,
of inner dawn.

Week One

Still Point

Hearing the call, becoming who we are

On 3 June, we keep the feast of St Kevin, hermit, monk and founder of the monastery of Glendalough in County Wicklow.

It was said of him that his prayer became so deep that, on one occasion, he was so still a blackbird mistook him for a tree and nested on his arm, outstretched from his little cell in prayer. He remained in stillness until the eggs hatched, having prayed to God to do so.

As a Franciscan, I have great love for St Kevin and for the hallowed woods and monastic ruins he and his followers left behind. He is like an Irish St Francis of Assisi, who reminds us, as so many of the early Irish saints do, that another way of dealing with the earth and our fellow creatures is possible: a way of reverence, respect and gratitude for the richness and beauty of creation, a way that through prayer and meditation comes to know the Divine Presence holding all things in being through love.

This poem 'Kevin of Glendalough' came to me after a visit to Glendalough some years ago.

Daily Meditation

Breathing in: I know that all that is has come from love.

Breathing out: I will walk the path of love's calling in my life.

Repeat this cycle during your meditation practice. If you become distracted, just gently return to the breath without any negative judgement or agitation.

Kevin of Glendalough

Only after
finding the
forested place
of stillness
between
the lakes,
between
the worlds;
only after
all the words
had been
dropped,
though reverently,
like leaves,
upon
the woodland floor;
only after
the hands,
now worn,
wrinkled,
thin,
were gently opened
palm to sky;
only after
the hooded mind
was
emptied
of
all the

shadows
that seeming
are;
only after
the heart
let go the chains
of its own
forging;
only after the
breath
became the slow
foundation
of being;
then,
only then,
did the deep stillness
arise,
and the eye of prayer
open,
and the spirit
breathe
the embers of
the long-banked heart-fire
into blaze.
And then,
only then,
did the blackbird
of heaven
nest,

and lay its sky-blue
blessings
of resurrection
promise
upon your
branched
hand,
anointing
with song
the promise of
heaven
for new beginnings,
while you,
tree tall
and
stone still,
beneath the
bowed benediction
of the
oaks,
became
monk,
became
sage,
became
prayer,
became
you.

Week Two

Still Point

Grounding and Barefoot Brothers

Perhaps the question we are most often asked as friars is, 'Why do you wear sandals or go barefoot in all weathers?' Monastic and Franciscan tradition gives three answers to this.

Firstly, to ground us in this moment in recollection and to remind us that we are pilgrims on a journey, as St Francis said, 'abiding not long in one place'. In other words, it brings the realisation that our physical journey is a mirror of our spiritual journey. Secondly, we go barefoot as penance for our own sins and the sins of others and as a way of uniting our suffering with the suffering of the poor, the downtrodden and the dispossessed. Finally, we go barefoot out of reverence for our sister Mother Earth who is doubly sacred both in her creation and in her supporting the feet of Christ as he dwelt upon her.

It's also very interesting that many people nowadays are finding a return to being barefooted, at least for a while and regularly, as a good means of calming and grounding, especially when they are feeling overwhelmed. Children know this and are quick to shed their shoes and socks whenever they can, and right up to recently summer was a time for sandals if not fully bare feet.

The next time you are feeling the need to ground in the presence of God and be really in the here and now, try a slow and gentle walk in bare feet and perhaps unite some of the intentions mentioned above as you breathe in every step.

Daily Meditation

Breathing in: I feel my feet upon the ground.

Breathing out: I stand in stillness in the presence of the creator of all.

Repeat this cycle during your meditation practice. If you become distracted, just gently return to the breath without any negative judgement or agitation.

Week Three

Still Point

A Wild Corner

*Praised be you, my Lord, through our sister
Mother Earth, who sustains and governs us, and
who produces various fruit with coloured flowers
and herbs.*

St Francis

St Francis always taught that our gardens should include
a wild, uncultivated place where the flowers and herbs of
the field could find a home and where we could rejoice in
their beauty and rest in their praise of the creator simply
by their very being.

May the garden of your heart always have a wild corner
where unexpected beauty and deep healing may be found,
inviting you into the joy of knowing that in your very being
you are called to be a blessing.

Daily Meditation

Breathing in: I greet the wild corners of my heart.

Breathing out: I rest in the uncultivated grace of the present.

Repeat this cycle during your meditation practice. If you become distracted, just gently return to the breath without any negative judgement or agitation.

Wood Walking

When you walk the woods,
do so at their pace.
Not yours.
Pause before you enter their embrace,
and breathe deep.
Slow down to their ancient pace
of root, and branch, and story.
Then, with a bow, enter;
and allow their cathedral coolness
to enfold you, and their greened light
to anoint you with sylvan sacrament
of stained glass dappling;
and your healing will begin.
As over the craggy
bare nerves of your busyness,
and sharp exhaustion,
and the rough edges
of your broken heart,
a gentling of moss
will begin to grow
as slowly as blessing.

Feel their tallness stretch you.
Their deep dark womb you.
Their leaf, and flower, and nut
circle you, with knowing,
of a kind unknown to
fleeting minds and
restless-hearted humanity;

greening you to
wholeness again.

Passing into their sanctuary,
stop; and become
one with them.
Let them teach you their
communion mystery;
their secret homing of
rustling life that
feathered sings
and furred shelters,
both beneath and above.

Listen long enough
and they will teach you
their tongue:
words of wood, and weather, and water,
united in one song of praise
that began with the first
divinely led step
into the dance of
inter-breathing
that you have forgotten
how to sing until now.

Sit your tiredness down
in the crook of their
rooted gathering,
with your back trunked;

and let them be your spine,
just for a while.
Your sap will rise with theirs
in the fourfold benediction
of the treed seasons
which foreshadowed
their glorious gifting
of their own element
to be the rood throne
of the Word
by whom all is spoken.
Touching their great slowness,
be reborn of their wisdom
that promises,
for every winter, a spring,
and roots deep enough
to outlast any summer drought
until autumn's coolness comes.

When eventually you rise
from their embrace,
stretch to the heavens
and breathe deep
of their largesse,
while ground gripping
with toe tap-root.
Their knowing, now with you
once again, will dust you golden
like pollen falling in the breeze.
Then bow deeply to your elders

and fellow servants
and walk back to your life
now luminous once again.

When you walk the woods,
do so at their pace.
Not yours.

Week Four

Still Point

Realise Love

In the end, we realise that everything that is
arises from infinite, unconditional, Divine Love.
We come from that love and are on a path of return to that
love.
The path of return is the path of learning to live from love.
You do not need to frantically seek love to possess love, to
control love.
You are already loved just by being you.
You just need to realise that every instance of love you
experience in this life is simply meant to be a reminder of
the infinite love that already holds you in being.
Breathe deep.
Rest in that love today.
Grow in that love today.
When anxiety calls, remember,
the foundation of your very existence is love.
Anxiety, worry, stress,

these things will come and go
and come again.
Beneath them all, behind them all is the simple truth: you
are loved.
This is the primary reason for the incarnation of the Word,
for the life, death, resurrection and ascension of Jesus;
to show you just how much you are loved.

Sacred Pause

Where do I need to allow Divine Love to bring healing and
peace in my life? How can I yield even more each day to the
transforming power of God's love?

Daily Meditation

Breathing in: I know I am the creation of love.

Breathing out: I will love myself as the child of Divine Love.

Repeat this cycle during your meditation practice. If you
become distracted, just gently return to the breath without
any negative judgement or agitation.

Sunday, Full Stop

Do not be afraid of stopping.
To pause and draw breath
is an ancient art
of wholeness and holiness.
Too often we travel piecemeal.
Our minds, hearts, bodies, souls,
taking different routes, different ways,
moving at different paces.
Just because I seem to be here,
does not mean I am.
I could be in a million places,
feeling a million feelings,
passing through the present fleetingly,
on my way into pasts long gone
and futures that may never be at all.
So practise stopping.
Pause a while along the way
and catch up on yourself.
Let your breath draw in
the sundered prodigal parts of you,
welcoming them home again,
without judgement or reprimand.
With each breath,
let them shuffle into place,
like a child in a school crocodile,
shoving, just a little, until
every one has enough space.

Then, whole again, for a while,
smile, and take one more step
towards the only destination there is,
the one who *is* love.

Midsummer Moonrise

Twilight breathes in me
as lady moon, our eldest sister,
rises over the fairy thorn.
I pause awhile and rest,
letting go day's burden,
welcoming night's wisdom,
I step into the between
and the becoming.
Step into the edge space;
the place of storied land,
ancient earth and even
heaven's blessing.
There, I am re-minded
that we truly live
between life and death,
between in-breath and out-breath,
between was and will be;
here, now, in this sacred place
of Divine Love's gifting,
the precious present moment.
Awareness, like the moon, rises
and casts her clear light
across the dark land of my life
and makes all things silver,
all things shine again.

July

Perhaps no Franciscan saint is as universally beloved as St Anthony. Though he is often reduced to the master of heaven's lost property office, in his day he was a miracle-worker, healer, renowned preacher and mystic.

Though he longed his whole life simply to disappear into prayer, his call was one of preaching and teaching throughout Europe. Indeed, he walked so far on his preaching tours that when modern forensics examined his relics recently, they were astounded to discover that he had worn his heel bones away on his many barefooted journeys.

No matter how far he went, though, he always took time to sit in silence, finding small caves, forgotten chapels and woodland glades where he could follow his breath into stillness and prayer. It was from this prayer, this abiding sense of God's presence, that the fire and power of his words came.

Finally, towards the end of his days when he could no longer travel, he had the brothers build him a treehouse hermitage where he could escape the crowds and contemplate in peace.

Anthony Ascends

His long travelling days over,
there is now only one direction left;
up, or is it, perhaps,
more truly, in?
The hilltop hermitage
was not high enough
to discourage those
who would still
seek his words,
disturb his deep prayer,
his long-sought peace.
So now the boughs
beckon him higher
to a cell, a nest woven
between the branches
by the brothers.
This is his place now;
held halfway between
heaven and earth.
What matter?
His heart has lived this way
all his life;
now the rest of him does so too.
Here, finally, the weariness
of the world may be dropped,
as he, worn out from roads
and crowds, and even from miracles,
climbs just a little nearer
to the clouds.

His body, almost too frail now
to hold heaven's fire.
Still, there are glints
of golden flame along the edges,
in his flashing eyes,
in his measured movements,
or on his tongue
as it tells the hours
in psalming whispers.
He is now,
a prophet become a burning bush,
a priest become a burnt offering,
a brother following the seraph song
all the way to heaven's vestibule.
He leans his back
against the trunk,
sits still and slowly fades.
A brown-robed grey-friar,
a hooded crow, upon the branch
as weather-beaten as the wood
on which he rests.
His chapel vault,
an arching branch.
The greening sunshine
through the leaves,
his stained-glass window.
His choir, the birds.
And he who has learned
at last their song of innocence
hears, understands, and smiles

at their skyborn summons.
From here he will ascend,
this sylvan stylite,
and will be ever after known,
and busied even in eternity, as
Finder of the lost things,
Friend of the poor ones,
Pilgrim preacher of peace,
Brother to the sisters
in their needs.
But for now, at least,
there is a moment's rest,
here upon the hillside
under the passing sun
and moon,
beneath the branches,
and breeze-played leaves,
above the earth,
alone, at last,
where all the words
are dropped
like leaves
upon the wind,
Anthony
simply
is.

The Importance of Halfway

Halfway is important.

It can be a place of rest,
a place to catch up with each other,
to gather ourselves,
to pause and look back,
remembering with joy
the gifts of the past,
and, of course, its lessons,
hard learned, perhaps,
but now wisdom
that we have grown into,
and could not imagine being without.

And so here,
at the halfway mark,
we invoke the inspiration of the spirit,
who first set us on this journey,
breathing in once again
the energy of beginning,
and, perhaps,
taking a moment
so as to reorient ourselves,
to that inner light,
that guides us on our way.
Halfway is important.

It can be a place from which we look forward
into the mystery of the future.
It can be a place to make plans;

to feel again the excitement of the explorer
looking down the road to all the un-named places
yet to be visited.
Or perhaps,
we glance ahead
with the fear of the one
who looks into the unknown with dread;
and imagines trials and pains ahead,
that make the journey
so burdensome
it may never even be begun.
And so here, at the halfway mark
We invoke the presence of the Son,
Who has promised to walk
just ahead of us, always,
turning our path into pilgrimage,
and,
allowing faith to flower fully
as we come to know
we are never alone
upon the road.

Halfway is important.
It can be a place to rest
and come home to ourselves.
To dwell in the now of this moment;
this sacred moment,
receiving it with joyful gratitude
as
a holy place,
In which we simply are

what we are:
Brothers on the road
together.
And so here,
at the halfway mark,
as sun sets and moon rises,
We invoke the presence of the Father,
Who is our origin and our destination;
the place
in which we dwell,
and the path
on which we travel.
The one who offers us
in goodness the gift
of this holy halfway moment;
to breathe, together
to pause, together
to praise and pray, together
to remember, together
to plan, together
to be, together.
And from this halfway moment
to know again
that Spirit-filled,
Son-led,
and Father-loved,
we may always make
any moment,
even the halfway ones,
a place to begin again.

Week One

Still Point

Making a New Beginning

In the sayings of those extraordinary early monastics and contemplatives known as the desert fathers and mothers, men and women of great faith who transformed the wastes of Egypt and Lebanon in the third to the fifth centuries into centres of prayer and contemplation, we read that 'Abba Poemen said of Abba Pior that every day, he made a fresh beginning'.

St Francis too used to say to his brothers each morning: 'Let us begin again for, up until now, we have done so little.'

To know that each day, indeed each moment, possesses the possibility of beginning again in the love that *is* God is the beginning of the true path of the conversion of the heart.

To begin to draw into our awareness the grace of knowing that each day, each morning, each moment, each breath is a Divine invitation to begin again and to offer this gift of new beginning to all those we live with and those we encounter upon our way.

Daily Meditation

Breathing in: I choose the grace of dwelling in the present moment with Divine Love.

Breathing out: I choose to begin again in this sacred moment.

Repeat this cycle during your meditation practice. If you become distracted, just gently return to the breath without any negative judgement or agitation.

Week Two

Still Point

Retreat Skies

You can make a retreat anywhere. You don't need to travel in any direction but inwards. Divine Love awaits you in your inner room, your soul space. To withdraw, simply follow the path of breath, gentling yourself in stillness, remembering that you are the mountain of your retreat. Your heart the cave at its summit where God's Holy Spirit dwells. Your thoughts, your feelings, your worries, your stresses are all just weather; clouds, simply passing by. Abide in the cave. In the stillness of the sacred place, between in-breath and out-breath, and soon the sun will shine on the mountain once more.

Daily Meditation

Take some moments to breathe. Simply notice the rhythm of your breath without trying to change it in any way.

Breathing in: I withdraw to the cave of the heart.

Breathing out: I abide here in peace.

Repeat this cycle during your meditation practice. If you become distracted, just gently return to the breath without any negative judgement or agitation.

Dawn Sitting

To sit
in
stillness
as dawn
wakes,
is a
sacred joy.
Keeping watch
as
first light
illumines
the heart's
altar,
calling it from
its
flickering
candled
dream-darkness
into the
now
of
awake awareness
is to dwell within
a
daily resurrection.
Sitting still
I allow
Divine attention
to

breathe blessing
through me
upon the
hinge
of
the morning,
so as
to watch
its door open
within
to Divine Light
and
then,
I begin again,
in love.

Week Three

Still Point

Lean Back

Lean back.
Lean back into the embrace
of Divine Love.
You are the visible crest of a wave
travelling over a deep ocean of love,
so what have you to fear?
Lean back into the presence
of all the holy ones gone before;
known or unknown,
of all times and places;
they support you,
surrounding you on your way
as a forest surrounds
the smallest sprouting seed.
There is not one of them
who does not daily
will the full flowering of life in you.
Lean back into their strength.

Lean back into their love.
Lean back into the deep river
of the ancestors
from whom you came.
However they lived then,
they offer, at the very least,
wisdom as to how to be now.
Lean back into their stories;
the dancing entwinement
of their lineages
has brought you forth,
has clothed you
in flesh and blood and bone.
In your body
a thousand generations
walk again upon the world.
In your eyes
a unique soul gazes
out upon the world.
Lean back into all those
who have made you, you;
parents, siblings, family, neighbours,
friends, lovers, colleagues,
the passing encounters of a moment,
the deep connections that last a lifetime,
they all travel with you.
Did they bring you joy, light, love?
Then give thanks,
for they have taught you how to be.
Did they bring you sadness, darkness, pain?
Then give thanks,

for they have taught you how not to be.
Lean back into the enormity
of the vast spaciousness you are,
a being in time meant for eternity,
a being of body, mind, heart, soul,
a being never alone,
a being of love's holding in being,
a being coming from love's creation,
a being returning to love's embrace,
a being who in every moment may
lean back into Divine Love.

Daily Meditation

Breathing in: I accept the wisdom of the past.

Breathing out: I let go of anxiety about the future.

Repeat this cycle during your meditation practice. If you become distracted, just gently return to the breath without any negative judgement or agitation.

Week Four

Still Point

From Ordinary to Extraordinary

'*A spirituality that does not transform is a false spirituality.*' This was one of the favourite sayings of one of our older brothers. It is a reminder to all of us that our meditation and prayer must penetrate to every part of our being and activity. Even the simplest of acts, like washing up or setting the table, can be done with such grace, mindful attention and good humour and that the kingdom of God can be revealed while working side by side at the sink.

Bring your spiritual practice to the ordinary and it becomes extraordinary.

Sacred Pause

Happiness – real, consistent happiness – is not about the big ecstatic moments that come and go, often leaving a stunned, exhausted void of longing in their place.

Instead, it is a choice made every day to slow down enough that you may deeply notice how every moment and experience, even the so-called 'negative' ones, are teaching you that you live in a world filled to the brim with amazingness and wonder.

True happiness is the realisation that breath by breath, little by little, we are waking up to just how loved we are and just how wonder-full creation is.

Daily Meditation

Breathing in: I choose to be fully present in each action today.

Breathing out: I rest in the grace of the joy at the heart of creation.

Repeat this cycle during your meditation practice. If you become distracted, just gently return to the breath without any negative judgement or agitation.

Late Summer Morning

Late summer glows golden
with watered-down sunshine,
washing greens transparent in gentle grasp.
Wasps in sulphur yellow drone heavy,
and trees tinge flame as
loose leaves begin to tremble
at autumn's edge.
The last swallows dip low in frantic flight,
feeling the old way they will follow soon
in damp dusky air.
Blackbird flutes clearly
dawn's daily retreat and tonight
harvest moon will redly rise.
All as seasons' four-spoked wheel turns
around the still centre of Divine Love.

August

Mantras of Meaning

A mantra is a sacred word or phrase that may be used in our prayer and meditation as an aid to focus. Though we use the Indian Sanskrit word '*mantra*' to indicate such a practice, it has also been present in the Christian tradition where it was known as the *versiculum* or 'prayer word'.

The word is repeated, combined with the breath, in order to allow the person of prayer to remain consciously in the presence of God, who is always present to us. At different times and for different reasons, our mantras may change as life goes on. We see this in the prayer of St Francis, who across the course of his life, worked with three *mantras* that can inspire our own prayer too.

I

'Who are you, my Lord, and what am I?'
This was the mantra prayer of Francis at the beginning of
his conversion and inner journey. It is something I return
to again and again. For in its answer is everything we are
and could become. It can be our prayer too as we begin
again in each day and even in each moment.

II

'My God and my all' (*Deus meus et omnia*)
At the midpoint of his life as he entered into the illuminative
stage of the mystical journey, Francis saw that all is in
God and God is in all. I whisper this as prayer, as hope, as
longed-for light that I too may see all as it truly is, all as it
exists in God.

III

'Peace and joyful goodness' (*Pax et bonum*)
Now the fruit of the journey is born as transformed by the
love of the one who *is* love, the fountain of the Holy Spirit
overflows and Francis bears the fruit of his prayer.

Meditation

What would my mantra or *versiculum* be that asks of God the deepest questions of my life? What word or words will I use to unite my breath and being in conscious awareness of God's loving presence?

Breathing in: I attend to the presence of God.

Breathing out: I let go of all distraction and anxiety.

Repeat this cycle during your meditation practice. If you become distracte, just gently return to the breath without any negative judgement or agitation.

Week One

Still Point

The Sanctuary of Slow

Slow down.
Just
slow
down.
Slow to the pace
of the shifting clouds,
of the sun and the moon,
of the great long cycles of the
stars,
of the earth
as she
holds
and
sustains
you.
Then
pause;
deliberately

and
deeply.
Rooting yourself
in
your
breath
as the
guardian
of the
doorway
to
the sanctuary
within.
And then,
enter the
infinite space
of
this present moment,
as it
opens up
before you.
Finding
therein
endless possibility
and
the awareness
of
infinite,
unconditional,
Divine
Love.

Pouring
into your heart,
into your world,
moment by moment
and bringing
peace.
Remember then,
each day,
with each breath,
that all you
have to do
is
simply
slow down
and you will
touch
the
real
and discover it
as
love.

Daily Meditation

Breathing in: I unite my breath with the meditation word.

Breathing out: I abide in the word and the breath.

Repeat this cycle during your meditation practice. If you become distracted, just gently return to the breath without any negative judgement or agitation.

Week Two

Still Point

Come to Stillness

> *Be still and know that I am God* (Ps 46:10).

Sit in stillness,
rest in your breath,
close your eyes to distraction,
allow your mind to dwell in your heart,
your inner space of love where Divine Love abides.
Then you will perceive the gentle movement and call of
the heavenly dove whose inner light will penetrate your
darkness, whose song will call you home to yourself,
home to the embrace of Divine Love.

Reflection

As the psalmist who wrote so many centuries ago reminded
us, be still and you will know. What will you come to know?

The presence of Divine Love holding all things in being. We can bring this wisdom of the psalms or, indeed, of any piece of sacred scripture to our prayer and meditation by using its gentle repetition as an anchor for our presence in stillness and peace.

Daily Meditation

Breathing in: Be still and know.

Breathing out: That I am God.

Repeat this cycle during your meditation practice. If you become distracted, just gently return to the breath without any negative judgement or agitation.

Week Three

Still Point

Assumption Eve Medicine

In many places, it was the ancient custom for women to gather herbs around the feast of St John the Baptist (midsummer) and bring them to the churches for blessing on the feast of the Assumption on 15 August before they were made into medicine for the winter ahead. The herbs were placed beneath the altar cloths and around the sanctuary before the dawn mass in order to be offered to the Lord through Mary's hands, she who is the 'first fruits' of his saving love, to receive her special prayers of healing and be blessed in their medicinal use in the year ahead.

The ritual of the church still provides for such blessings should they be requested.

One of the oldest principles in the ancient healing art of monastic herbalism is that the plants would only give up the fullness of their healing virtue when combined with prayer. It was a wonderful reminder that healing, however it comes, has its ultimate origin in God's love for all people. It also reminds us that the full virtue not just of plants but of all beings is only seen when we approach them with love and attentive prayer.

Daily Meditation

Breathing in: I invite God's healing love to journey to every part of my being.

Breathing out: I pray that I may be a healing presence in the world.

Repeat this cycle during your meditation practice. If you become distracted, just gently return to the breath without any negative judgement or agitation.

Assumption Eve Medicine

For two months turning,
the old women,
they who have the knowing,
have watched their charges carefully.

Picked at the height of their power
on the short night, after the long day;
the feast of fire,
that vigils the Baptist's coming,
when lads and ladies leap
like hares over flames
and look with longing for love,
as children sing the old songs
filled with mystic meaning;
that night they were gathered
as grace and gift
beneath the light of sister moon,
the Lady's lamp, and plucked
from garden and from forest glade,
by woman's hands alone.

Now they, the herbs for healing,
hang in blessed bunches
over the hearth of home,
or kept in kitchens
above the range,
or bound in byres
where the warming breath
of the queen kine keeps them

charmed and waiting
to release their medicine,
the healing pulse
of sister Mother Earth
and brother sun's distilled light
mixed and married and greened,
in root and shoot
and leaf and flower.
So they, the healing herbs,
have rested until tonight
when as dusk comes on
and begins to breathe her
autumnal quickening,
these wise ones take them down
and bring them now
to the old places of prayer
to the abbeys and chapels,
to the candled shrines
of the sainted ones,
who themselves bore
the fruit of blessing
and were heaven's healing,
the salve of souls,
upon the earth.

There they find
the Lady's chapel,
and lay their leafy burdens
beneath the linen cloths
upon the altar, there to await
assumption's dawn,

and as the mass bells ring
to have the holy words
said over them that render
them thrice blessed again,
and ready to release their
gentle healing gifts,
blessed once in very being
from first beginning's breathing.
Blessed twice in the burning
touch of love's own resurrection light
when all was made anew.
Blessed thrice by the Lady's prayers,
she who is the stock from which
all healing blooms,
and in her gathering home raised all
that grows green upon this good earth
to become heaven's healing help again;
Eden's elixir restored in her
and birthed anew as grace,
just as these sainted herbs
ground upon the mortar's stone
will give their essence up,
and become the holy way
by which their medicine
blesses bodies and anoints
our souls to ready us
in our own time,
for heaven's
homing.

Catching Your Breath

Come,
sit a moment with me
by the road
and catch your breath;

Or rather,
let your breath catch up with you,
from the place you birthed today
as you woke.

For, rushing into the day you left her behind,
alone,
a sacred whisper stirring from sleep
at the deep pace of growing things.

Too busy to hear her call
you have been without her,
exhausted but searching,
panting and gasping and empty.

Gently now, receive her back
into the sanctuary of your heart
and allow her to take her throne
there once again.

Remember then,
to walk slowly and deeply
into the rest of the day,
at the slow pace of breath.

For you do not want
to lose her again,
and feel only the panicked absence
of her grace,
all while being pulled into
the maze of before and after;
where she never truly dwells anyway;
except as a stranger
seeking your return.

For she is the guardian of your soul
and she dwells
only here, only now,
in this precious moment,
a gift of divinity,
hallowing the temple of our being
and uniting us
with the Divine now.

Come, sit a while
and catch your breath.

Week Four

Still Point

Putting the Pebble to Your Lips

It was said of Abba Agathon, one of the great monastic teachers of the early church, that for three years, he carried a pebble around between his lips until he learned to be silent.

Sayings of the desert fathers

We live in a world of noise and so forget that our words have an energetic weight for good or bad; that they carry a moral weight. To learn silence is to come to know the power of our words and so to choose them wisely.

Put the pebble of mindful silence to your lips.

Pause before speaking.

Feel the weight of your words.

Then, we will become aware of the Word who *is* behind the silence, speaking the cosmos into being through love.

Speaking through us if we are silent enough to hear.

Daily Meditation

Breathing in: I rest in the stability of my own breath.

Breathing out: I choose to anchor myself in the present moment.

Repeat this cycle during your meditation practice. If you become distracted, just gently return to the breath without any negative judgement or agitation.

Mobile Meditation

When the mobile phone
went off
right in the middle
of the meditation,
there was a wave of discomfort
you could nearly touch,
as the lady who brought it in
desperately tried to silence
its summons.
One could almost hear the inner questioning
around her:
Did you not see the no-phones sign outside?
Did you not think to check
your phone was on silent?
Though truth be told,
in the midst of the inner tutting was
another thought:
I am so glad it was not my phone that went off,
and
Is my phone on silent?
How long before I should check?
Only the monk smiled
and at the end of the meditation,
to the surprise of all,
bowed to the phone owner
and thanked her
for revealing to us all
the depth of our distraction:
'Many of you were not really here,

but the ringing brought you back.
Many of you leapt to judgement,
so the ringing revealed
the real depth of your compassion.
Many of you became concerned
about your own phone going off,
so the ringing revealed the depth
of your attachment to self.
How precious was that distraction
for what it showed you of yourself.
How precious are all distractions
when they reveal
to us how far we have travelled
away from our
practice, from our
prayer.
How precious they are,
if we consider them
to simply be
shining signposts
on the way of return,
on the way
home.'

Autumn

Falling into Autumn

Autumn brings with it the wonderful combination of flower and fruit and gilded leaf. Everywhere there is colour and largesse. From the hips and haws of the hedgerows to the fiery leaves and fruits of the forest, there is an almost overwhelming explosion of energy. Every plant seems to be competing in its channelling of fire. The annual cycle of the four seasons comes to its completion with harvest and hope before the rest of winter quiet.

For me, the gift of autumn is seen most splendidly while walking in the woods.

Growing up, I lived near an old beech wood. It was beautiful all year round of course but, in autumn, it sang. Silver trunks, golden leaves and the rich, rust tones of the beech nuts on the forest floor made a wondrous tapestry to walk through in the early-morning sunshine; while visiting the wood during September nights to see the badgers and foxes about their ancient rounds allowed one to see the trees tall against the stars and straight as ancient columns gilt by a golden harvest moon.

Even the student melancholy of a return to academic life was mitigated by marvelling at the colours of the ivy on the buildings and the search for conkers among the fallen leaves.

For the contemplative there is so much to attend to, to be mindful of, in this season that one must start small. Take some time with an individual leaf or tree. Pause often on your way and listen to the wind or the songs of birds as the dawn chorus begins to find its way back after the quiet of the nesting season.

The feasts in summer and autumn are very Franciscan in tone: the feast of St Clare (11 August) in August's edge days between summer and autumn leads to the Archangels on 29 September and Francis on 4 October. The whole spectrum of creation tuned to Divine Presence that transcends the sensory view and mounts towards heaven, spurred on by the gift of beauty all around – this is our practice and our community in these autumnal days.

May the still points and poems of these autumn months invite you into wonder at the grace of beauty all around you and then into gratitude for the harvest of meditative awareness they offer.

Lady of the Autumn

Our Lady of Autumn,
queen of the mists
and of the dreamtime,
I call you.

Mother of the falling leaf,
the red berry,
the ripe fruit upon the branch,
and the soon-sleeping earth,
I bow before you.

You who are
our twisted roots'
autumnal fruiting;
bringing long-hoped-for harvest,
where
bare branches
once stretched skywards
and,
in their naked yearning,
past storm and struggle,
prayed,
longed,
for the seed
of new creation
to be planted.

The song
of earth's ancient desire

fills your silence
and meets in your
surrendered heart
its psalmist
where,
in answer to
your song of yes,
the seed of spring
is planted
in
your high-hedged field,
and the promise of
summer
is heard,
even in my
sin-wintered soul.

Pray for me,
mother of mists and moonlight,
that I,
oft fog-bound
and fruitless,
will find in you,
always,
the seed that dies not
but gives,
even lately and lastly,
spring flowering,
and,
at the end

of all the beginnings,
a harvest
that no winter
may wither.
Amen.

Elijah and the Way of Abiding in Stillness

What do you think of when your hear the word 'prophet'? For most people the word conjures up images of a sort of divinely approved clairvoyant. But, in scripture, a prophet is less someone who can tell the future and more someone who can read the present. A prophet is one who enters the present moment so deeply that they discover there the presence and action of Divine Love.

The prophets were sent to advise people about how they should act in the now. Again and again, they are sent to the people, from the kings to the lowest reaches of society, to assist them in discerning the will of God and in following it fully. Even the Hebrew word for prophet expresses this wonderfully, *na'avi*, meaning 'one who sees deeply'. The charismatic gift of the prophet, often born of long-life dedication to meditation on the word of God, was to be able to see the hand of God where it is active, in the now, as opposed to merely seeing it after the fact, as most of us do.

As the great theologian and now saint Cardinal Newman often said: 'The action of the Holy Spirit is only seen in retrospect.' This is true for all of us ... except the prophets. Nowhere is this most beautifully mapped out for us (as many of the great mystics have recognised) than in the story of that greatest of Hebrew prophets, Elijah, who taught us how to listen for God in the present moment, how to attune our attention mindfully to the one who is the I AM ...

Found in the First Book of Kings (19: 1–15), the story of Elijah, the greatest of the Hebrew prophets, is that of a man consumed by zeal for the Lord and for the faith of Israel. Coming out of the desert as a man on fire for the Lord, he is sent to call the people of Israel back to the faith of their ancestors. Recognised as the greatest of the prophets next to Moses, he even appears in the New Testament in the person of John the Baptist, who comes in the 'spirit and power of Elijah' to prepare the people for the coming of Christ and is seen, along with Moses, on the mountain of transfiguration speaking to Jesus as he prepares for his passion and death.

But even this greatest of prophets can lose touch with his vocation for a time and come close to despair. When we read of these moments in the lives of the great teachers, it should come as a relief to us, for it makes them human just like us and subject to the same doubts and worries that we can often give way to. The way in which God calls them back to their true self often provides a map for us when we too get lost or stuck on our own journey or even simply experience ongoing difficulty in sustaining our prayer practice. This is particularly true of the story of Elijah, which Christian monastic teachers have used again and again to illustrate the path and practice of attentive, mindful prayer.

We begin by finding Elijah under the threat of a death sentence from the king for having insulted the royal dignity and accusing him and his wife of idolatry. This sentence seems to destabilise Elijah at the core of his being. Even though he has seen the marvels the Lord has worked through him up to now, fear, anxiety and the seeming pointlessness of his mission to call the people back to the Lord begin to overtake him. Elijah appears to lose touch with his calling and, with it, his meaning and purpose. His focus wanders away from the place where God is –

the present – and he gets lost in anxiety over the future (catastrophising as he ruminates on the threat of death), and in rumination over the past ('I am no better than my ancestors'). Feeling himself unconnected from the Divine Presence by becoming lost in his own thoughts, worries and anxieties, Elijah touches despair and goes into the desert to lie down and die. Here, we see a man spiritually exhausted, touching real depression and even perhaps suicidal despair.

We are told in the Book of Kings that he chooses to walk into the desert. Walking into the desert was a gentle way of committing suicide at that time. You kept walking until you were overcome by heat exhaustion and then you simply lay down and slept your way to death. Those reading Elijah's story in the deserts of the Middle East would have been very clear about what was being indicated by his journey into the desert. Both metaphorically and literally, Elijah, overcome by anxiety, fear, stress, exhaustion, rumination and sadness, has nowhere to go and no energy to move. We can see the story already speaking to our world at this time too, can't we?

It is precisely at this moment of crisis that a word from God is offered to invite the man back into being a prophet. An angel appears. Not with glory or trumpets, but with food and drink. The angel touches Elijah on the shoulder and shows him a scone of bread and some water, the simplest of foods, the simplest of drinks. 'Get up and eat', he is told. Not just once, but twice. It's a very ordinary miracle, and yet it says so much of the tenderness of God.

God gives us what we need in the moment. No more, no less. And, in that moment, our despairing, depressed prophet needs to eat and drink. In the moment of his pain and sadness, God asks no more of him than that he would look after himself.

There are many lessons in this miracle that our monastic fathers and mothers have seen over the years of their *lectio*, their spiritual reading of the text.

Firstly, we see the importance of making sure that our basic bodily needs are met prior to beginning the work of meditative prayer (or we will simply be thinking about them rather than praying, as anyone who has attempted to pray when hungry or tired will attest). Secondly, we see the importance of the eucharist for our life journey has been hiding symbolically in the food and drink offered to Elijah. Finally, we see the simple wisdom that, when a brother or sister is despairing of practice and the faith or even just lost in depression, the bodily needs for companionship, food, drink and rest are the best of cures.

For us, though, examining this story as an archetypal map for the practitioner of attentive mindful prayer, what do we find in this simple angelic offering? Elijah is invited out of his anxiety and rumination, out of the future and the past and is set back on his feet in the present moment by the simple, grounding action of eating and drinking. There is much wisdom in this alone. But the story goes further. Elijah the physical being has received sustenance but now the heart of the prophet must be renewed too and he is sent further into the desert to Horeb, the mountain of God. Now, with the gifts of the angel and receiving from him both direction and goal, the desert that was only a short time ago the place of despair and death becomes a place of encounter and call. Elijah journeys for 40 days and 40 nights into the heart of the desert. He recovers in his own person the 40 years of wandering of his people. The symbolism of the 40 days would not be lost on Elijah nor on our monastic fathers and mothers. To journey into the desert for 40 days is to journey to the place of contemplation where our own being, detached from all of the distractions of the past and future, may rest in the silence of the interior desert where every bush is aflame with the fire of God. Elijah journeys to the place of encounter with God. To the mountain where God revealed his glory, his light to Moses.

Arriving at the mountain, how must he have been? Worn out and tired? Perhaps. But there is an exhaustion that accompanies the work of the moment, the simple carrying out of what needs to be done, that is a healthy and satisfying tiredness that would have seemed so different to the lassitude of despair and anxiety.

But Elijah is not ready to touch Divine Presence yet.

He goes first to the cave. Symbolically, this is always seen to have been the cave of the heart. Elijah rests in a real cave on Horeb but enters the cave of the heart, the place of sanctuary at the heart of our humanity where God dwells. But he is not yet ready. We see this as, having come to physical stillness, his anxiety and fear, his ego and distracting thoughts all waking and showing themselves. He must sit past them all to come to Divine encounter. Elijah demonstrates to us the simple power of abiding in attentiveness. He has been told to wait for the encounter with the Lord, with the great I AM, as God had revealed his inner name to Moses in the burning bush.

Elijah's role in this is simply to wait. Our role is the

same: to wait past everything that will arise within us until our heart is quiet enough to know the presence. Be still and know. So Elijah waits.

There are three great manifestations that take place on the mountain of meditation, and the teachers of our tradition tell us that these three great movements will take place in us too when we sit in meditation. Let's look at each of them.

The first manifestation is a great wind, sometimes translated as storm or hurricane or whirlwind. But the Lord, we are told (the I AM), was not in the wind. The early monastic writers saw in this the manifestation of the thoughts that arise in the practitioner, all of the distracting, often crazy and even weird thoughts that our mind fights stillness with – the *logisimoi*, as the desert monks called them, the thoughts that are like mosquitos; huge in number and exhausting to fight. So how do we deal with them? Elijah shows us. We simply abide in mindful attention. We do not fight them or grasp them. We do not feed them with our attention. We look through them or beyond them just as we would look at a beautiful landscape through a cloud of mosquitos. When we do not feed them, they disperse as we discover, just like Elijah and all the practitioners before us. The Lord is not in the whirlwind.

The second of the manifestations that takes place is the earthquake. But the Lord, we are told (the I AM), is not in the earthquake. This may be viewed in two ways. Firstly, as we go deeper into our prayer life we may find that our inner sense of who we are begins to break down. This is a good thing. All of the egoic illusion that we have constructed around ourselves, the false and often prideful narratives that allow us to compromise with the spirit of the world or the attitudes that see us as being better than others or the petty jealousies and even the old wounds we have suffered, all of the hidden darkness within will be broken up and brought to the light of Divine Love for healing. Without this happening, our prayer will always have something of the false ego about it. The second major earthquake that takes place is the realisation that God is infinitely bigger than any idea or image I have of him. Eventually all images of God must be let go if we would truly allow God to be God and encounter his presence. This too can feel like an earthquake for the practitioner of mindful attentive meditative prayer. Both of these movements can be frightening and may even put off some practitioners as their life circumstances may need to be questioned by this step. But if we are to stand on a firm foundation in life and for eternity then this breakup, this earthquake, is needed. However, this emerging sense is a reaction within us to meditative prayer, and while it is used by God, it is not a perception of the Divine Presence and so must be encountered wisely, with guidance from the community and the tradition. Too many who encounter this movement beneath their feet run to action without wisdom and hurt themselves and others in the process. In our moments of prayer, when this sense arises, we are simply called to notice it but to keep our attention on waiting for God. Elijah shows us. Abide in attentive prayer. For the Lord (the I AM) is not in the earthquake.

The third manifestation that takes place is the fire. This is often translated as a raging fire. It's a good translation as this, the ancient writers tell us, is the fire of desire. Now, we are not talking about sexual lust here, that is just one of the desires. We are talking about desire itself.

We are talking about the need to grasp, to possess things, people and even God as though we own or control them. The fire is only seen after the first two manifestations as it is so much a part of our fallen psyche that we must practise a long time even to be aware of the deeper ones within us.

Now, let's be clear: desire in and of itself is a good thing. All of our hungers are meant to be fed appropriately and have their ultimate satisfaction in God. It is when desire is unrestrained or gets caught up with false ideas and egoic pride that there is a problem. For example, the human hunger for love is a good thing and takes us out of selfishness and into generosity of spirit and growth and expansion of soul, but a desire for love that exalts personal need for love over the needs of the beloved, such that they become an object to be used rather than a person to be related to, or that sets limits to their growth so that I will not have to change and grow myself, is a truly negative thing for both parties.

Fallen selfish desire makes the false self the sun in the solar system of relationships with people and things, and slowly consumes all with its fiery heat.

When this form of desire manifests itself around God and faith it is truly terrible as it spawns an idolatry of self that allows us to dictate to others who God is (we remake God in our own image and likeness, shrinking him in the process), and this, in turn, spawns ideologies of hate and fundamentalism. Revelation and sound theology are relegated and downsized to proof texts with which I can score points over the other, instead of being seen as the invitations to the contemplation of Divine truth and mystery they actually are.

Through the fire we must journey, and we will find remedial action for these desires in the grace of the sacraments and in the practices of mortification and penance, as well as generous and compassionate service to others. But in the moment of prayer, our duty is simply to abide past these false and idolatrous notions, letting them fall away and burn themselves out until they are silenced. Again, Elijah teaches us how. Abide. Be still. Wait on the Lord. For the Lord (the I AM) is not in the fire.

The three archetypal manifestations have been sat through. Elijah has not been distracted. He has kept his attention, his *prosekai*, his *kavannah*, his mindfulness, on God. He has seen through the thoughts, he has accepted the earthquake, he has allowed the fire to burn itself out and he is delivered now to stillness, to the moment of the contemplation of Divine Presence.

There came the sound of a gentle breeze, we are told. The rabbis and monastic commentators tell us that this may be equally translated as a sound of murmuring silence or even the sound of gentle breathing. It contains all of these sacred senses, and, with it, comes the understanding that it had been there all along but was being drowned out by the noise of the false manifestations and the anxiety and the regret and rumination.

On hearing this sound, being attentive enough to discern it, Elijah covers his head (a sign of reverence before the Divine Presence) and goes before the Lord (the I AM). This is why we sit. This is why we abide past the noise. This is why we do not cling to the past or the future.

This is why we allow the wind to blow itself out, the very seeming foundations of our life to crack beneath us, the fire of unrestrained desire to be consumed by itself. We abide in sitting to come to the sound of silence. We abide in sitting to come to awareness of the gentle breath that sustains all that is. We abide in sitting to come to stillness. We abide in sitting to become still and so to know.

Elijah knows now. He is, once again, *na'avi*, the prophet, the one who sees. His contemplative encounter sets him back on his path, as it always does. He knows now that the future and the past are in the hands of God and all that he must worry about is the duty of the moment, for that is the call of the prophet. Whether he lives or whether he dies in the carrying out of the mission is immaterial. There is no false self between himself and God now for he has heard the sound of silence, the sound of the Divine in-breathing at the heart of creation, he has heard the word and zeal, for the Word will consume him.

It will consume us too if we allow it, if we find the still point beyond the noise of our broken being and surrender there to the love that *is* God. This is the mindful path of our attentive prayer, and the Lord, through the story of Elijah, greatest of prophets, gives us our map into mindful mysticism.

Meditation

Breathing in: I choose to be present to this moment of grace.

Breathing out: I share the peace of this moment with all.

Repeat this cycle during your meditation practice. If you become distracted, just gently return to the breath without any negative judgement or agitation.

September

Often seen as a liminal time of transition, with the chill of autumnal nights struggling with the days of late-summer warmth, September is a good month for us to begin again after the sometimes more disorderly days of summer travels and school holidays. Let it be a new beginning to your practice if needs be or, if not, then a deepening of what you are already doing. Sit with its contrasts and notice how each day, each moment, is different. Though they arise from the same Divine source, they are unique, and, when gone, will never come again. Let September teach you the joy of noticing the changes around you and the unchanging gift of Divine Love.

September In-between

This is the season of in-between,
a sacred door into the dragonfly days
of sun-blushed berries,
and fruits full upon the branch,
when autumnal fire crackles
slowly over leaves,
unleashing light along their veins
tempting them towards
the tension of windborn wonder.

These are the days of swallows and starlings
gathering as slow storm clouds
before their flocked flight warmwards,
screaming their farewells,
fountaining forwards,
free upon the foaming clouds.

These are the days of first noticing
the chill and the dark,
though not as winter yet,
only as remarked change upon our skin,
walking from patches of conversation
into silent introspection,
feeling the old summons of schoolday beginnings,
the burgeoning pull-tide of term
we never truly escape from,
no matter the outer age,
that calls our shuffling feet towards
the first drifting leaves and

makes us count conkers upon the trees,
even if our pockets hold other treasures now.

These are the days of longing,
yearning for those sunsets and mornings
just now out of reach,
that teach us the deeper soul longing
for love's eternal summer,
yet we rejoice too
in the brittle sharp newness
of lowering sun and rising moon.

These are the days of hunting,
of homing, of harvesting;
of gratitude given before the gathering,
of berried blessing being
between us and all that is,
and though our gaze now looks
long towards winter
we dance here, now,
in the days of autumnal grace,
the days of in-between.

Autumnal Nuns, or *Nunc Dimittis*

While journeying between activities
alert only to radiophonic babble
I passed through a place of trees
and was caught out of time –
entered the deep bronchioles of branches
a forest of fireworks static against the sky
and admired the feeling of sad awe they started from a heart
filled with tiredness –
I saw, of a sudden, two old nuns ...
The one tall and thin and head above the other
pre-shrouded in a grey overcoat,
a distant-destination look in her eye.
The other making small steps alongside
as a tug to a tanker or a moon to a planet.
So they walked in a timing of a long time created
and now lapsed into easily,
like snug slippers or broken-in boots
and no word passed between ...
Why?
What thoughts passed between these weather-beaten bodies
sundried fruit faces
and yet, shining eyes?
No need for speech when all has been said.
Or when silence is reached as a goal and not an escape.
In drift of fallen firework sparks they walked
yet shone in my mind all the brighter,
these secret sisters;

treasure chests opened, but not with human key ...
Soon to be joined with earth and air and water ...
Dissembled and yet
shining still as stars erupt into night sky.

Autumn Equinox

Last night,
as the half moon
rose
in a purple cold
and star-frosted sky,
the lady autumn
knocked
upon my door.
Flame coloured
and
berry beautiful;
she left
just one
token
of her
passing presence:
a
leaf,
rubied by her
fiery touch
and blessed,
now,
into brittle beauty.
Scribed upon
its parchment
was
her
season-song:

'All things change,
but nothing dies
and by their ending
all things begin.'

Then I saw
how
seed and leaf,
flower and fruit,
all
circle past,
but
are held
in
sainted cycle
by
love's presence
until
the Lord
of
time's circling
comes again;
and in his
seasons' summoning
brings
fruiting
and
flowering
together

into
one
eternal
moment
of
love.

Week One

Still Point

Feast of the Holy Name of Mary

Names indicate nature and calling in scripture. The name of the one called to be the mother of God is no different and means 'full of light' or 'bringer of the light'.

Both senses are present in the greeting the Archangel Gabriel makes to Mary. He calls her full of grace (literally 'the light and life of the Holy Spirit').

All of the other names and titles given to Mary all stem from this first naming and show that when we open ourselves fully to God's love and plan then we become the temple of his presence and a locus of grace and blessing wherever we are and in every need.

Sacred Pause

Let us be true to the name of Mary and become ourselves, through our prayer and good works, people who are full of grace so that we may in turn become, through her help, true to the name of Christ and find our own inner name, our inner meaning, in his name, the name of God's love.

Daily Meditation

Breathing in: I invite Mary to be present in my life.

Breathing out: I say 'yes' with Mary to the will of God for my life.

Repeat this cycle during your meditation practice. If you become distracted, just gently return to the breath without any negative judgement or agitation.

Week Two

Still Point

Transcending our Wounds

In 1224, while keeping a lent (a fast of 40 days) in honour of St Michael the Archangel, St Francis withdrew to the mountain of Alverna and lost himself in meditation.

In prayer, he petitioned God for two graces: that he would feel in his own person, so far as humanly possible, the suffering of the Son of God for all creation and, secondly, that he would feel in his own being, so far as was humanly possible, the infinite love of God for all creation.

These graces were granted when, on the feast of the Holy Cross (14 September), he beheld a vision of a seraph beneath whose wings was revealed the crucified Christ. After the vision, Francis found that he had been marked with the stigmata, the visible wounds of Jesus, in his hands, feet and side, thus becoming the first to experience this mysterious gift in a visible manner.

Daily Meditation

Breathing in: I choose to be present to the changes autumn brings around me.

Breathing out: I offer the harvest of my breath and being to Divine Love.

Repeat this cycle during your meditation practice. If you become distracted, just gently return to the breath without any negative judgement or agitation.

Stigmata

That morning
the people woke
to a mountaintop on fire.
A red gold dawn
seemed to forget
the ancient bounded truce
between heaven and earth,
and, descending, christened
the forested crown
with flame.
They wondered then,
what had become of them.
The small band of brothers
who had passed through
barely a month earlier,
begging their way
towards the foothills
lost in the mad heart song
of faith, of Divine desire.
Seeking the solitude of spirit
that only the wild bestows
as blessing.
They were three,
and another one
they did not come
to know,
cowled as he was
in smiling silence,
yet with the look of loss

about him,
as though he did not
live fully
now upon this land.
Sometimes, later,
if the wind blew aright
they swore that
in the starlit silence
of the night
they could hear them singing.
They felt sad then,
as you do for those
you do not really know.
To be lost on a mountain
in a forest fire.
How terrible!

They did not listen to the child
whose piping voice asked
insistently
why there was no sound
of burning,
no stampede of the furred
and feathered
from this strange flame,
but only light and silence
and a stillness
until then unknown,
except, perhaps, before
a summer storm,
or sudden fall of

winter snow?
The child was shushed,
they always are;
and sad and solemn

words were said,
and then the business
of the day began.
Eyes averted by all
except the child,
who stood and
stared long
and, finally, smiled,
as the others' faces
turned towards
the ground
of ordinary hours,
fell into the
forgetfulness of fire,
as we so often do.
And when, by chance,
they looked again
they saw now only
a September sky
over a forest turning
autumnal gold,
and thought, *well now
we must have been mistaken,
a rare dawn, no doubt.*

Some days thence,
the brothers came again,

thinner for their mountain days
yet seeming wrapped in wonder
and singing as they walked.
Save for him,
the silent one,
bowed and bent around
an inner burden
none could see
but all could feel.
His hooded face
unseen,
they all kept their distance,
fearing the mad
contagion of faith, perhaps.
All, that is, except the child,
who found him sitting alone
beneath a tree
and offered him
the raw innocence
of her unflinching gaze.
He smiled at her then,
as, with the noble courage
of her age she said,
'They thought you burned in the fire.'
He lowered his hood,
she saw his hands then,
their centres
splashed with scarlet
and with iron
from which a golden flame

now sparked, as though
the light of heaven,
earthed in him,
could not be contained
in such a vessel,
small and broken
in his fiery blessing.
'I did,'
he said,
'I did.'
And then they laughed
a while together,
and, singing,
both went forth
to play.

Week Three

Still Point

Centre and Edge

God is that whose centre is everywhere and whose circumference is nowhere.

St Bonaventure

Reflection

Tuning in to the Divine Presence can be hard. It's like trying to pick up a radio or wi-fi signal when there is lots of interference. We need to create space and time to attune ourselves to be aware of what is already there. What are the noisy places in your life that keep you from tuning in?

Take a few minutes each day without background noise – no phone, no TV, no internet – then simply relax your body, sit still and for five minutes invite the Holy Spirit to reveal the Divine Presence around and within you. Deeply notice all that enters your awareness through the senses. Breathe deep and breathe love!

Daily Meditation

Breathing in: I choose to be present in the presence of God.

Breathing out: I let go of the mindless noise in my life.

Repeat this cycle during your meditation practice. If you become distracted, just gently return to the breath without any negative judgement or agitation.

Week Four

Still Point

Close Your Eyes

Close your eyes
and,
following
the ancient path
of breath,
come to rest
within yourself,
and
find there
the
still
centrepoint
of
perfect peace
where
Divine Light
dwells.
Abide there,

in
open-hearted
attentiveness,
and
make your
dwelling
in that
infinite
spaciousness
that exists
in
the
eternal now,
between
the
in-breath
and
the
out-breath,
and,
once
there,
become
love.

Daily Meditation

Breathing in: I choose to be present to the wonder of the ordinary.

Breathing out: I choose to allow the grace of the now to enter every aspect of my being.

Repeat this cycle during your meditation practice. If you become distracted, just gently return to the breath without any negative judgement or agitation.

Autumnal Art

Autumn truly gets under way in October.
This is my favourite time of year.
when the trees become rainbows,
and sister Mother Earth gives back all that she has
received,
changed by her magic art
into fruit and berry and nut,
each holding the power and blessing of the summer sun
to sustain our strength in winter darkness.
A reminder that all we receive as gift is only ours if we
can let it go ...
Not just once,
but
again and again ...
changed and charged with love,
the fruit of compassion
offered in thanks to the one who, in love,
is the
original giver of every gift.

Autumnal Wood Wisdom

Enter
slowly,
and with reverence,
the golden
autumnal woods,
and then,
stopping
beneath
its vaulted
sylvan sanctuary,
allow its
burnished beauty
of
bronzed leaf,
polished nut,
and
shining fruit
to reflect deep
eternal richness
of
Divine generosity,
always
gifting grace
in each moment,
of heaven's harvesting,
to breathe its blessing
through you.
Then,

accepting its
annual invitation to
stillness,
you will
hear
the slowing
heartbeat of the earth
as she moves towards
her
yearned-for yearly
time
of
maternal meditation,
and feel her
ever-deepening breaths
appear as
mother-mists,
exhaled
between branches
slowly releasing
leaf's attachment
into wind's wildness,
beckoning you
into the stillness
that bears
always
the slow-fruiting
berry
of

prayer,
whose
bittersweet taste
is
wisdom.

October

The month of October has always been beloved to me, holding as it does the feasts of so many saints, the remembrance of the Rosary and even the spooky wisdom of Hallowe'en, but, for a follower of the Franciscan way, it is very special indeed. On the third of October we celebrate the *transitus*, the passing into eternal life of St Francis, and then on the fourth we celebrate his feast day.

Perhaps no other saint has so fully gripped the imagination of humanity, regardless of religious tradition, as St Francis has. I have found him to be loved by Christians and Buddhists, by Hindus and Muslims and Pagans alike. Perhaps his message of the brother/sisterhood of all being allows him to be a sacred door through which all may enter and encounter his heart, a heart totally dedicated to Christ. This dedication led him along a path of prayer and meditation that allowed him to drop all that was not Christ from his mind and soul. This way of joyful detachment is a central practice of Franciscan meditation to this day. In the words of Francis, 'to hold back nothing of ourselves for ourselves, that the one who has given himself totally to us may receive us totally.'

Whatever the reasons for his connection with so many, Francis continues to call all people to be instruments of peace to one another and to care for all of creation as a wonderful manifestation of Divine Love and beauty.

May the following poem, arising from my meditations in Assisi at the hermitage of one of Francis' first and most beloved followers, Brother Leo, help you to come to know St Francis as the brother to all people and all creatures he is.

Brother Leo Remembers Brother Francis

'What was he like?' I asked,
exhausted from my climb to pierce the
cold clifftop cloister of
this cowled brother's retreat,
hoping to stir to remembrance his soul
first stung by the seraph's fire so long ago,
yet burning still in eyes ancient but clear
that gazed upon my lack of grace with mercy,
and smiled at me from a distance I cannot fathom.
'What was he like?' he whispered to himself,
holding my question as carefully as the jug
with which he poured me water, cave cold and clear,
to quench a pilgrim's thirst.
Then on that hill above Assisi
the old hermit friar spoke,
slowly at first, and stumbling,
as though his tongue, long lost in silence
of cave and forest, had now to stretch itself
and awaken language once spoken long ago,
like one who comes home from a foreign shore
and finds now the accents of his own confusing.
So we sat before his cave he and I,
friar and novice both,
lost in legends and lore,
all the more beautiful for being
at the same time,
truth;
and needing to be told once more
to a world longing for his possibility to be made present

in Edenic blessing
once again.
'What was he like?'
'Like a tree he was,
that on summer days shines green
and in its topmost branches feels
the waft of heaven's winds
and dances even at the stillest hour,
or that in autumn clings not to leaf
but
changes loss to gift by
casting clothes windwards and
delights in lightness,
its bare bones describing sky
and pointing arrowlike
always upwards.'
'What was he like?'
'Like a stone he was,
smoothed by the sweet rain,
graced by countless hours of chiselling prayer
into a solidity of stillness.
A cornerstone, a keystone, a foundation stone
able to hold the weight of wisdom lightly,
yet bear up the broken and bridge the gap;
a stepping stone to wholeness and home
for those long lost.'
'What was he like?'
'Like the night sky he was,
open, and sheltering, and many-
coloured in magnificence, but
starlit in simplicity.

Its beauty simply a gradation of light,
infinite in scope and eternal in origin.'
'What was he like?'
'Like fire he was,
tracing his storied path from spark to ember,
even in stillness, a banked flame,
and always energy of exultation breathing blessed,
a conflagration of communion,
buried just beneath the ashes of abstinence.'
'What was he like?'
'Like a stag he was,
who knows where the sweet water flows,
and travels the deep dark valleys
and mountain crags to reach his slaking spirit stream.
'Loud as a bear he was,
and as quiet too,
spending his winters between
wakefulness and sleep,
lost in the cave of the heart,
barely breathing,
but
murmuring mercy for all,
until spirit spring stirs and his
honeyed roar was heard again
upon the hills.
'Like a wolf he was,
singing soul songs beneath sister moon's gaze
with clear eyes lost in heaven's love,
calling to himself his pack, those
who heard their song and soul sound
in his echoes of emptiness.

'Badger brawny and
filled with faith's wisdom he was,
and, likened to old *broc*,
he knew the ancient ways and
night-walked, as they do,
secret silent paths of prayer,
long trodden, but needing
refinding always, in each
generation's journey.
'Like a salmon leaping he was,
glittering like glass,
light sparkling from sliver scales,
struck by sunlight, suspended
between sky and stream in a
moment of stillness
over ever-rushing river.'
'What was he like?'
'A living song spark wrapped in the
nest of Mother Earth,
enfolded in the dun dust-brown of the sparrow,
small and thin he was,
with a barefooted skipping gait
barely holding the joy that burst from his breast,
his cross-feathered soul
never far from song.
'Like a wren in a thornbush he was,
cocking its eye wryly at the earth-bound,
certain of its power of flight
and yet choosing our company.
'Like a robin he was,
who, tree hidden from view,

sings its piercing song of heaven,
drawing down remembrances
of innocence past
into tired hearts sure they were
long past childhood's delight in sheer being,
and there waking wonder once again.
'Thin like a thrush he was,
who seeks the highest branch
even in storm, and sway-sings with delight a tone made
purer
for the assault of wind and rain
and thunder crackling all around it.
'Like a hawk he was,
staring with unblinking eye into love's light
and falling like a stone from heaven
to shock his sleeping prey awake.'
'And now?
What is he like now?'
'Like a lark he is,
free and flying heaven high
whose sun-kissed song
seeks only an open soul and then
beckons all skywards.
'And I miss him, though
he sings his lark song in my heart too.
Aye, and in yours as well or you
wouldn't have visited me here,
now would you?
'But I shall fly to him soon,
and there we will sing together
once again our lark lauds for the one

who gathers all, bird and beast and brother, in blessing.'
And then we sat, old and young together,
cowled in brown both, though centuries between,
and ghosts to each other,
meeting in eternity's one moment,
until the sun set and the moon rose
waiting for the nightingale to chant her compline call
and Assisi bells
to ring out again
in midnight matins
his song of peace.

Reflection

Take some moments in nature this month to truly see the beauty around you. Go outside if you can and allow all your senses to gently receive the blessing of Divine Presence in and through the gift of creation.

Meditation

Breathing in: I am part of God's creation and have a responsibility to preserve its beauty.

Breathing out: I am a brother/sister to all beings.

Repeat this cycle during your meditation practice. If you become distracted, just gently return to the breath without any negative judgement or agitation.

Week One

Still Point

The Little Way is the Mindful Way

St Thérèse of Lisieux was a Carmelite mystic and doctor of the church. She passed to the Lord at only 24 years of age having attained in her short life, the fullness of mystical perfection. Her spirituality was based on her 'little way' – bringing the love of God into each succeeding moment and in whatever activity she was called to, remaining inwardly present to him. Thus, even suffering and pain became transformative when it was encountered.

She is often called the 'Little Flower', a title that belies her extraordinary inner strength. The next time you hear her called thus, be aware that a flower that knows where the sun is will crack concrete to get to it over time.

May we follow her in her dedication to Divine Love and compassion in each succeeding moment.

Sacred Pause

*If I did not simply live from one moment to another,
it would be impossible for me to be patient, but I
only look at the present, I forget the past, and I take
good care not to forestall the future.*

St Thérèse of Lisieux

How would it be if I followed the 'little way' of living from
moment to moment in the presence of God's love?

Daily Meditation

Breathing in: I choose to be present in the here and the now.

Breathing out: I choose to live this moment in love.

Repeat this cycle during your meditation practice. If you
become distracted, just gently return to the breath without
any negative judgement or agitation.

Week Two

Still Point

Breathing Peace and Joy

In St Francis of Assisi, we find one who passed through the work of meditation and reached the heights of contemplation.

He passed from his first prayer of conversion – 'Who are you, my God, and what am I?' – to the prayer of creation itself: 'My God and my all.'

Seeing deeply within and beyond every being he encountered, he beheld the Divine Light of the love of the creator, holding all things in being and continually pouring itself out in unconditional love for creation.

Recognising the common origin of all beings, he was invited into the universal song of praise that is the very energy by which all things exist. And there, encountering them as brother or sister, he became their voice, their minstrel and their herald, liberating the secret gospel of creation present in their very being.

His mission then was to remind sin-sundered humanity of their origin and destiny in the Word who *is* love and who pours himself out for them upon the cross that they might take their place as brothers and sisters, sons and daughters of the most high and follow the way of *pax et bonum* ('peace and joyful goodness' in Latin).

Daily Meditation

Breathing in: Who are you, my God?

Breathing out: Who am I?

Repeat this cycle during your meditation practice. If you become distracted, just gently return to the breath without any negative judgement or agitation.

Wind Waltz

Enjoy the beginning
of the annual autumnal
dance
of the leaves
today.
Watch them wind-waltz
towards the earth
as blessings
carrying
within them
the seeds of next
spring's
waking.
Let them
be a
wonderful reminder
that endings
always
hold beginnings
at their heart
and that
the great lesson
of the
resurrection
is
everywhere
for those
with eyes
to
see.

The Melancholy of Autumn

Travelling through the season of mists,
I drove,
of a moment,
into a cloud of melancholy,
waiting for me
upon the road.
And briefly,
for just a moment,
I dwelt in its depth of deadness,
and sweet, sorrowful, calm,
where no noise comes
and no outside word is spoken.
Accelerating away
I felt its fingers, freezing,
seeking my heart's warmth
so as to wake in me
all that I have lost,
or never gained.
But I,
breathing deep,
chose once more
the springtime dawn
of
each moment's
new beginning,
and
invited in the light
that dissolves
all darkness.

And so,
I drive on,
facing forwards,
and,
glancing in the mirror,
I see now no mist.
But there,
upon my cheek,
I feel,
like fog condensed,
a single tear.

Week Three

Still Point

Passing from Death to Life

In 1226, worn out by his labours and knowing his end was coming close, St Francis asked the brothers to bring him to the little chapel of Our Lady of the Angels, just outside Assisi, so that he could pass to the Lord under the watchful care of the blessed mother to whom he had entrusted his own life and the order he was leaving behind. Commemorating this event, we Franciscans gather every year, and in song, chant, reading and reflection meditate upon the way of his passing and the teaching it brings.

Transitus

All holding,
grasping, desiring,
had long been
given up.
What was left now,
but only the fear
of leaving
them behind?
Even this,
he knew,
must be
given away
as gift.
So he did,
smiling
at the face
of his sister,
death.
Then, as a
dandelion seed
upon the
breath breeze
of a child,
he
let
go.
Becoming, finally,
what he had
always wanted

to be:
a dancing
wish
on the
wind
of
God.

Reflection

In our meditation moments, it can be good from time to time to remember our passing, whenever it will come. St Francis suggested we should greet death as our 'sister', one who comes to care for us and allows us to follow her into the freedom of eternity. While we may not be that ready to think about death like this as yet, we can at least in our meditation begin to cultivate the understanding that all things are passing.

Daily Meditation

Breathing in: I remember there was a moment when I experienced my first breath.

Breathing out: I remember that there will come a time when I will experience my last breath.

Repeat this cycle during your meditation practice. If you become distracted, just gently return to the breath without any negative judgement or agitation.

Week Four

Still Point

The Mindful Bow

In both the East and the West, one of the most important practices taught to monastics is that of bowing.

It is meditation in movement and, when done mindfully and with deep awareness and breath, it has the power as a practice to bring all of the mental, physical and spiritual faculties together in one action of unified attention.

We bow simply in greeting or profoundly to mark moments of deep grace when we are visited by Divine Love in the liturgy, in prayer and meditation, or simply before the beauty of creation.

It is an act of vulnerability and humility in which the monastic acknowledges that we are not at the centre of the universe, we are not the most important, we are simply a mirror reflecting back to the other their Divine origin and seeing in them the presence of Divine Love and compassion.

We acknowledge in the other their unique giftedness, their necessity of being for the completeness of the kingdom. Bowing says, *Let me learn from you, be open to you, listen to you, recognise in you the hand and voice of the Divine teacher.*

Bowing empties us so that we might be filled.

It is an act of thanksgiving for, and solidarity with, the other. Even when we disagree with the other, we can come to silence and simply bow, reverencing the best in the other, seeing them as a sacrament of Divine Presence, even if their view is opposed to ours.

Leave aside words, look deeply at them as brother or sister, and bow. At a time when so many refuse to give or yield or acknowledge the needs and rights of others in the world, perhaps the simple wisdom of the monastic bow needs to be learned again.

Today, profoundly, let us bow to one another.

Daily Meditation

Breathing in: I enter the silence at the heart of my being.

Breathing out: I breathe peace.

Repeat this cycle during your meditation practice. If you become distracted, just gently return to the breath without any negative judgement or agitation.

All Hallows' Eve

This was the evening she swept out the hearth.
I helped, sort of.
Once clean, and perfect to her discerning eye
(milky white, though the light behind them was sharp and
never dimmed),
she would set bread – brown soda always – and salt before the
banked flames.
'For the visitors,' she would say, whenever I asked,
as I did, annually.
Her breath whistling half-heard prayers,
she would go then from room to room
straightening cushions,
flicking tables with tea-cloths,
to clear the last vestiges of dust
from surfaces so well polished
with age and use, they gleamed.
'The house should be clean when they call,' she would say.
We would have tea then.
Waiting.
Sometimes she had cake or a ginger snap
(dunked to soften it for dentures).
I had cake too.
Then she would sit in her stiff-backed chair
in front of the fire.
Waiting.
I would sit beside her,
sometimes in the big green armchair
slowly sinking into the old feather-filled cushions,
so big my feet swung.

More often, I perched on the stool beside her chair
where I could watch the TV with her.
But not this evening.
This was always different.
No RTÉ news.
No *Crossroads*.
No *Coronation Street*'s plaintive trumpet.
Just sitting together in the quiet.
Waiting.
Tonight there would be just the fire,
and the bread and the salt left out,
blessed and prayed over and freely given
for the guests,
whenever they would come.
And then she would talk about them.
All of them.
Her mother and father, her aunts and uncles,
and tales of Dublin so long ago it seemed
they should begin with 'Once upon a time'.
Her grandmother got special mention:
'They called her a sharp woman, wise,
brought in for birth and death, you know;
she had the understanding,' she would say,
and then say no more for a while.
Sometimes,
she would speak in a different voice reserved only for him,
of my grandfather Martin, her husband,
gone an age ago to me,
but still so present to her heart.
Then her eyes, looking across the flames at faces I could not
see,

would bring to mind all those others too
who had already gone …
and she would go quiet.
'Where have they gone?' I would ask.
'Home,' she would simply say.
But tonight, they would visit.
Once, just once,
it made me nervous to think of it.
She laughed then.
'Nervous of the dead?
Don't be silly.
Aren't they family?
Aren't they friends?
Don't they pray for us!
Don't we pray for them?
You can fear the living,' she would say,
a sharp smile playing about her wrinkled eyes, 'but never the
dead.
A Christian never has to fear the dead.
Sure don't we have the Blessed Virgin and all the saints
around us too.'
Then she would take my hand and we would just sit.
Waiting.
She praying …
I wondering …
Feeling the wrinkled warmth of her loose-skinned hand.
Safe.
Then she would suddenly say
it was time to go home.
So I would go then, across the green.
Home to parties and noise

and black-bag-wearing, apple-bobbing,
door-knocking, sparkler-waving,
'Help the Halloween party!' roaring fun.
Sometimes I would think of her.
Sitting in front of the fire.
Waiting.
But mostly I didn't.
Until the morning,
All Saints Day.
Off to mass, a day off school too.
Then, in the afternoon, I would drop over.
To find the telly on,
the chair turned now to face it once again.
The bread gone,
salt scattered to bless the house and garden.
'It's Richard, Gran!' I'd shout.
And I would hug her and tell her all about it;
the parties and the sweets, and the things we called wine-
apples
because we didn't know what a pomegranate was,
and the lady who always gave rotten brazil nuts you couldn't
crack
(last Christmas leftovers we were sure!),
and she would laugh and make the tea,
and we would sit again,
side by side,
and wait for *The Two Ronnies*
and then, I would remember and ask
(during the ads, of course),
'Did they come?'
'Oh yes,' she would say, 'they always come.'

'What do you do when they come?'
'What does anyone do when visitors come?'
she replied, with a slow smile.
'You chat?' I'd say.
'Exactly,' she glittered.
'Now be a good boy and turn up the telly.'
And I was, so I would.
A quarter of a century has passed
since she went home.
But still, this night always,
I welcome the visitors too.
Friars and family both now.
Sitting before the candle flame
breathing the blessed breath
of memory and prayer.
Waiting.
Just as she, my first elder, taught me.
Waiting.
She now, always
a visitor too.

All Hallows

The earth has offered up
her harvest.
Now,
broken open,
after birthing bounty,
breathing deep
she slumbers.
The trees shiver shower
their leaves
to cover her nakedness
and dance a lullaby
in the brittle wind
while whispering songs
of winter's coming.
And so,
we weak ones
draw near to each other
around the old hearth,
long hallow'ed by story,
and there tell the tales
of before,
and between,
and behind,
pressing so close
that we feel comfort
in their holy presence
and,
against the dark,
within more than without,

we kindle grave lights,
scatter salt,
and break bread
in invocation,
and keep the
month of memory,
while
mother sleeps
into spring,
and remembers when
her child and father both,
in one word,
descended
and
twice took refuge
in her womb
and there,
sowing seeds of saints,
began
an
eternal spring.

November

In the Catholic tradition, the whole month of November is dedicated to praying for and remembering the dead. We begin with Hallowe'en, the eve of the feast of All Hallows or Saints on 31 October; this falls on the old Celtic feast of Samhain, which, again, was to do with remembrance of the dead and was seen as the time when the veils that separated the worlds of the living and the dead were at their thinnest.

This feast was subsumed into the Christian calendar from very early on. Prayers and rituals were offered for the departed and often a candle or light was lit specially in the home as a way of remembering those who had gone before, and this continues right up to the present day. In my grandmother's time, as described in the poem 'All Hallows' Eve', the custom was to clean the house and sweep out the hearth and leave bread and salt in a dish as the ancestors would come and visit the house on this night.

The feast of All Saints, 1 November, issues in the month properly with its remembrance of all the saints of all times and places. All those men and women who have lived lives based on compassion and goodness and who have been gathered together in the kingdom of heaven.

On this feast, we celebrate not just the canonised saints but also the common-or-garden saints, as one old priest I knew used to put it – all those who, though appearing to live ordinary lives, were transformed by grace and love to live extraordinary lives that brought peace and compassion to the world. The feast stresses that sanctity is the destiny of every human being and that it is within reach of all of us. In the churches, solemn masses and blessings with the relics and icons of the saints are offered.

The second of November is dedicated to the feast of All Souls; here we remember all of those souls who though departed from this life are still *in via*, on the way to God. On this day, we remember those souls who are completing their journey to heavenly life through the state of purgatory. We call them the 'holy souls', for their salvation is assured and they, in turn, can pray for and help the living, but we also call them 'poor souls' for they are dependent on our prayers, penance and acts of charity.

Prayer for the holy souls is considered an important way of offering spiritual alms, and so, on this day, every priest may offer three masses, and the Office of the Dead is prayed by priests and monks and nuns. The faithful attend mass, light blessed candles and visit the graveyards throughout this month. One beautiful custom, which, as far as I know, is only found in Ireland, relates the prayers for the dead to the falling of the leaves, in that if a leaf fell from a tree in front of your face it was taken to be a message from one of the holy souls asking for prayer.

In the Christian tradition, ghosts in the proper sense (not poltergeists or mere psychic impressions) are known to be souls in purgatory who appear to ask for spiritual help via prayer to complete their purgatory and move on to heavenly life.

The faithful also record the names of their departed loved ones on the 'November dead lists' and these lists are placed upon the altar and mass is offered for those whose names are recorded daily throughout the month. Special services of remembrance of all those who have died in the past year are held in most churches, with their families being invited to come back and light a candle for the deceased. The candle is then given as a gift of remembrance to the family that they can bring home and light to remember their loved one. In addition, people often fast from meat and/or alcohol and add extra prayers and daily attendance at mass for the holy souls.

Week One

Still Point

Soul

God created man in his image;
in the Divine image he created him;
male and female he created them.

Gen 1:27

The Lord God formed man out of
the clay of the ground
and blew into his nostrils the breath
of life,
and so the man became a living soul.

Gen 2:7

Nowadays, soul can often be seen as a word that deadens with its weight, rather than as an experience that vivifies with its presence. In Hebrew, the root language of the tradition to which I belong, there are two basic words used to describe the different parts of what we call soul:

nephesh and *ruach*. They mean very different things, but neither exists fully without the other to define it; and, in the dance of their relationship, we come close to discovering the unique and ancient insights that, when received fully, allow our understanding of what soul is to become utterly transformative and liberating.

However, before we get to the inner meaning of soul, we must abandon some concepts about our souls that too many of us hold without ever having examined them fully. They are a hangover from that period we call the 'Enlightenment', when soul and body were tragically separated with a Cartesian knife, an injury that has yet to be healed in the psyche of the West. Because of this philosophical butchering, when asked to describe what a soul is, the majority of us descend into images of ghosts inhabiting bodies. We speak of 'having a soul' in the same way that we have a dog or a father or a job. It is almost as though we imagine that, just as if we lost our pet, our parent or our employment, we should still exist independently (though saddened by the loss we have endured); so if we lost our soul, we should be fine, if a little less 'full'. Of course, nothing could be further from the truth. As the great C.S. Lewis was wont to remind his pupils: 'You do not *have* a soul, you *are* a soul.' The *I* that you are (beyond and deeper than the mere egoistic I), the individual expression of Divine creativity that is your unique presence in the world – this is your soul. The *you*-ness of you is the apprehension of your soul by your intellect.

So what is this soul-stuff that we are? For that we must go back to the very beginning again … to the dance of *nephesh* with *ruach*, of in-breath and out-breath.

In the Book of Genesis we are told in the most magnificent poetry just what it is we are. (We are the subject of poem and myth, all of it true, for the simple reason that myth and poem speak to our souls in ways that the dry digest of history never will.) So what are we told there? Simply, that our life is the result of Divine inspiration: we have been breathed awake. We *are* a living soul by virtue of this Divine in-breathing. We may live this earthly life, as the Chinese sages say, between the in-breath of birth and the out-breath of our passing, but we began as humanity through a Divine exhalation which granted life and movement and awareness of our relationships with God, with one another and with creation.

The mud-moulded mannequin of the Pagan myths awakens to its true nature in the Hebrew revelation that we are not that which perishes and dies; rather we are that which is called to respond to the creator as Father/ lover for eternity. The soul that is breathed into the human being is the *nephesh*, the creative power of God. It is not God, but, as the ancient monks and Hebrew mystics will realise through their inward encounter, it is a Divine energy proceeding from God and holding us in being. As we breathe we are held in the sustaining breath of God.

We are ensouled by Divine breath, by Divine life itself. God bestows the gift of *nephesh*, our individual personhood; our soul. Mind, heart and personality arise from the *nephesh*. So that there would be no mistake about the intimate and unique relationship that humankind enjoys, through its soul, with its creator, the ancient Hebrew sages and prophets went further and coined the word *ruach* to speak of the Divine in-dwelling at the heart of the soul. This is the utterly unique spark of presence, by which we are connected to God at the heart of our being.

Ruach is the in-dwelling spirit of God, the activity of God within us. The *ruach* of God dwells within us as the spirit of God dwelt in the temple. The one who hovered over the waters of primordial chaos and called forth order, harmony and beauty hovers too within the depths of *nephesh*, within the depths of our soul, in that place we call spirit, and, if yielded to, will call us into order, peace and harmony also. It is through allowing the action of the *ruach* of God within, that the image and likeness of God is gradually seen without. An image that, as we see from the scripture above, will be called forth from every human being regardless of gender, creed or colour.

So how do we come to know our soul? How do we yield to the action of the *ruach*, the spirit of God within us; such that our *nephesh* may grow and the image of God be revealed within us and so within the world? The answer is surprisingly simple ... perhaps too simple. It has been known since the beginning of time, but through the egoistic amnesia that we call sin, it is forgotten time and time again and must be relearned by the sages, the prophets, the monks and the mystics so that they may wake us anew to the full beauty of what we are in our essence. The answer is simply to breathe ... to breathe in a way that unites awareness with deep stillness and attentiveness, to watch what arises within and to cling to what is good while letting all that is not fall away from us. To align our breath with the Divine in-breathing is to align our being with Divine Presence. It is to enter the sacred desert within where even the bushes burn with the revelation of the God who *is*, 'Yahweh', the great 'I AM'. The one whose very name invites us to find him in the present moment where we anchor ourselves in the soul-space of breath.

'God is breath,' said the great St Maximos the Confessor, one of those who, like Elijah the prophet before him, went into the desert to discover the revelation that comes to those who persevere in stillness. They are those who sit in the cave of the heart until the storms and the hurricanes, the earthquakes and the fires of our emotions and desires have risen and blown themselves out. For then, they behold within themselves the revelation of the *ruach* of the spirit of God who comes to the one who stills themselves and who has learned the inner art of soul listening, like a still small voice, a gentle murmuring breath, a breeze upon the wind. Like the apostles who sat with Mary in stillness in the upper room waiting for the 'power from on high' that they had been promised by Jesus (the Holy Spirit he had breathed upon them and promised them a fresh outpouring of) – the Divine *ruach* that, when it came, arrived as tongues of flame and stormy winds that catapulted them into the streets to begin to wake the world anew to the 'good news' of the new creation that we are called to become – we will be called from our stillness to share the news of our soul – the image and likeness of God made visible in a world that is healed and renewed by the new creation – with all of those who hunger to know who and what they are.

So then, if you would know your soul anew, if you would step behind and beyond the brokenness of ego and the clinging attachment of desire to see the original beauty that God sees in you, then follow the path of breath and go inward into the inner chamber of the *nephesh* to discover the living soul that you do not *have* but that you *are* – and then go deeper still and in that inner sanctuary in stillness await the discovery of the in-breathing of the *ruach* of God that already dwells there, and know yourself to be a 'living soul', created in the Divine image and likeness.

Daily Meditation

Breathing in: My God.

Breathing out: My all.

Repeat this cycle during your meditation practice. If you become distracted, just gently return to the breath without any negative judgement or agitation.

One of the oldest prayers for the dead is the *De Profundis* (Psalm 129), which goes like this:

> Out of the depths we have cried to thee, O Lord,
> Lord hear our voice,
> Let thine ears be attentive to the voice of our
> supplication.
> If thou O Lord would mark our guilt; Lord, who
> would endure it?
> But with thee there is found forgiveness:
> For this we revere thee.
> My soul is waiting for the Lord,

I count on his word.
My soul is longing for the Lord
More than watchman for daybreak;
Let the watchman count on daybreak and Israel
on the Lord.

Because with the Lord there is mercy and fullness
of redemption,
Israel indeed he will redeem from all its iniquity.

Glory be to the Father, and to the Son and to the
Holy Spirit,
As it was in the beginning, is now and ever shall
be, world without end.
Amen

O Lord hear my prayer
And let my cry come unto you.

Let us pray.
O God the creator and redeemer of all the
faithful, grant to the souls of thy servants the
remission of all their sins, that through theses
pious supplications they may obtain the pardon
which they have always desired.
We ask this through Christ our Lord.
Amen

Week Two

Still Point

Support

Breathe deep,
be still,
then you will learn
that
every created being
is
supporting your
journey
into
the depths
of
Divine Love!
How can you feel
alone
when
the earth
herself
kisses

the soles
of
your feet
with
every step
you
take
towards
love.

Daily Meditation

Breathing in: I know I am breathing in (love).

Breathing out: I know I am breathing out (peace/love).

Repeat this cycle during your meditation practice. If you become distracted, just gently return to the breath without any negative judgement or agitation.

Week Three

Still Point

How, Why, When

The circumstances of our lives – the how, why, when and where we were born – are not of our choosing. But how we respond to these circumstances is. In that response is our call, our meaning, our hope and the encounter with the Divine transcendent, that we call God.

This response is both a life path to be taken and a moment-by-moment choice.

Remind yourself with each breath: in him we live and move and have our being, so the only response needed, at least as a beginning place, is gratitude for the moment, gratitude for the possibility of beginning again in love.

Each morning, practise beginning again by choosing to spend the first moment of wakefulness in a prayer moment of gratitude for the new day, asking the Holy Spirit to remind you of the deep possibility of beginning again with each breath, in each moment. A statement of prayerful, mindful attentiveness at the start of the day may act like our own powerful mission statement and may be returned to as a touchstone of practice throughout the day, renewing our awareness and our resolve. We can use a formal prayer of morning offering, or simply breathe and say something like:

I will trust that even my sufferings and problems will become moments of grace and learning as I dwell in them with full presence and awareness, knowing that the grace I need for each day is always present in the love that is God.

Daily Meditation

Breathing in: Today I choose to live awake and aware, dwelling consciously in Divine Love.

Breathing out: I promise to take time to notice the blessings that surround me and to choose the path of gratitude as I pass through the day.

Repeat this cycle during your meditation practice. If you become distracted, just gently return to the breath without any negative judgement or agitation.

Week Four

Still Point

God Is Love

To consider God as Love is to enter into all of the senses of love and there find Divine Presence. In God, we will find the ultimate fulfilment of our desiring, of the final object of all our affections and the satisfaction of our soul's yearning for completeness. All of the small day-to-day encounters with love in all its earthly forms become signposts to Divine Love. To name the inner nature of God as love is to affirm the fundamental reassurance that, amidst the messiness of life and behind the seemingly random event of our existence, there is an infinite, unconditional relationality that is drawing all that is into its embrace. St Bonaventure, one of the great Franciscan mystics and theologians taught that all that will ever exist proceeds from God so as to eventually return to God through love, love made visible in Christ. When through our mindful, attentive prayer, we begin to centre ourselves on this Love then all anxiety may be handed over in the precious present moment into the hands of Love and even the seemingly grey days of November begin to reveal themselves as moments of Love's revealing grace.

Sacred Pause

How would it be if I considered myself and others primarily from the position of God's beloved?

Daily Meditation

Breathing in: I choose to be aware of God's presence.

Breathing out: I let go of all anxiety and stress.

Repeat this cycle during your meditation practice. If you become distracted, just gently return to the breath without any negative judgement or agitation.

November Need

Each passing year,
I find I need November more.
Its time between is blessing;
a month of not yet but nearly,
when forests fade from autumn's
strident song of golden fall
to silvered fogs and frosted breath;
a clouded quiet month of middle distance
where vistas hide, or loom,
low-lit, from shadows,
and shapes dance liquid
in pools and puddles of reflected rainlight.
When dead and living dance closest,
and in fasting freedom feel each other,
as walls thin and edges blur
in mists and meres,
and our false firmness upon the earth
is shook a little further.
When we are offered the grey grace
of fogged futures, inviting trust
that behind the clouded sky, the stars, the hills,
the seas are all still there, waiting,
all held in an eternal gaze.
When hearts turn inward to memory's hearth,
feeding the flame of story with
the glow of back then,
and coals of gratitude spark
upon the inner eye,
while wisdom rises like woodsmoke

in sweet silence scented
upon the darkening night.
When quiet walks at twilight nip the bone
as cold finds its curious way between
the layers and makes the homing sweeter
for each lamp, each candle kindled warm;
all seeming to hold within the promise
of a longed-for rest at last, beyond all creeping cold
and chill.
When the thrill of all that's coming
begins to slowly steal in quiet moments
across the childed mind, and the winter chorus
of bird call and fox cry is herald heard
around the dusk and dawn as we
give ourselves to wait and watch for wonder's
warmth
to come again in December's carolled care.
But, each passing year,
I find I need November more;
a pause, a place, a prayer
before the blessed busy.
A time of breathing in,
not to be forgotten in its fading form,
but treasured as the place of waiting,
a seasoned hush upon the heart,
a sacred inhalation, a deepening,
a yielding to the velvet dark,
a softening into silence.

Lesson of the Trees

The tree lets go.
That is the lesson of November
and its last wind-dance of the leaves.
The tree always lets go.
It does not try to hold on
to spring buds,
or summer green,
or autumn fruit.
The tree lets go
of each, in turn,
and is not the less
for letting go,
but is, more so,
simply and beautifully,
in each perfect present moment,
the tree.

The tree lets go,
and by so doing
becomes stronger,
becomes taller,
becomes, completely,
the tree.

By following its
ancient
knowing,
engrained and
Divine drawn

in seed,
and twig,
and leaf,
and branch,
and every fibre,
it answers
the seed summoning
of love's first
in-breathing
and
grows greater
by
letting go.
By trusting
for strength,
in its
heavenward thrust,
the depth of
earth's mothering
embrace,
made from millennia
of
its ancestors
each,
in their turn,
letting go,
the tree rises.
So too
will our
being

become itself,
freely,
if we,
who so often
mourn
each season's
passing
and spend ourselves
in grief,
grasping our brittle leaves
of should bes,
and could bes,
and must bes,
always forgetting
that
within love's circling
nothing is ever
truly lost,
were
instead
to root ourselves
deeply in
Divine Love's
perfect present,
and then,
stretching heavenwards,
hear within
each season's summons
and,
simply,

like the tree,
surrendering to grace
and freedom,
to
let go.

Winter

The Peace of Winter

I have always loved winter. It is a season that could do with a little more love, especially in these northern climes where the oncoming of the dark evenings and the grey skies and frosted mornings bring so much stress and worry. And I get it, I do. I understand all of the difficult practicalities it may bring, but, behind all that, there is a beauty and, I feel, a deep contemplative invitation behind the quiet of winter that when entered into deeply and restfully rewards one with restoration and the touch of Divine peace. It is the earth's own season of retreat and it has many blessings to bestow for those who are open to them.

Many faiths take time to deepen their reflection at this time of year. Monastic communities often have periods of formal retreat during the winter months. It is a time to cultivate the deeper things and to rest as the seed in the earth and the bear in the cave do, trusting in the one who calls us into peace and who promises, after every winter, the possibility of spring.

One of my earliest winter memories is gazing up into an endless steely vault watching entranced as flake after perfect flake fell upon the earth and stung my upturned face gently with their cold kiss. My mother, who dreaded snow and ice, called us all back into the warm, but I just wanted to stay outside, looking up into this real magic that was happening before my very eyes, like manna falling from heaven.

This delight has stayed with me and has continued to deepen my appreciation for the gift of winter. Whether looking out at newly fallen snow, moonlit and glowing on our street or sitting in the forest hearing the bare branches sing their creaky song or listening to the flakes settle one upon the other, fitting together as surely as do jigsaw pieces, winter has a gift for teaching silence, for slowing us down and for inviting us inside – into the warmth, into lamplight and candlelight, into the cosiness of the fireside chat or the peace of the meditation rug or prayer stool.

The season of Advent, falling as it does at the very high point of winter days, is perhaps the most meditative of the liturgical seasons of the year, emphasising the need to abide in attentive, mindful awareness for the threefold coming of Christ: in history, at the end of time and here and now in this precious, present moment. It makes an already holy time of year even more blessed and promises us light even in the midst of winter darkness.

In the poems and still points of winter, may you find your winter dawns and dusks calling you with their sharper light into deeper awareness and restful abiding in the peace of the Divine Presence.

Daily Meditation

Breathing in: I gently accept the gift of winter.

Breathing out: I choose to hear the sacred invitations of this season.

Repeat this cycle during your meditation practice. If you become distracted, just gently return to the breath without any negative judgement or agitation.

Winter Sun

You may have
your languid summer skies,
all blue and cloudless,
they are beautiful,
in their own way,
I grant you.
But give me
instead
the sharp ferocity
of a winter dawn
flashing as a sword,
fleeting as the fast
glimpse of fox fire
between trees,
the quick conflagration
that pierces darkness
and hallows day,
and falls
upwards,
dragging hearts,
and land,
and love,
awake.
Sung skywards
with the mighty
choir of those
birdsouls
who lean forward
out of darkness

as lines are defined
in sharp shock
of brother sun's first
frosted touch.
Yes.
Give me a winter sky,
a dawn Divine,
an advent promise of
light beyond the dark
where every tree,
illumed and stretching,
writes a gospel upon golden air,
and the hidden holy is seen
as breath upon the icy breeze
announcing in whispered wisps
he came, he comes, will come again
like sun blast, sun burst, sun rise
of a winter's dawn.

December

My Gran and the Christmas Invitation

St Stephen's Day, December 26th, is very sacred in Ireland, no more so than in our family – not just because of the first martyr's witness and passing to the Lord, but because it is also my gran's anniversary. My mother's mother, she was (and is) one of the greatest influences in my life growing up and remains so to this day.

I have always regarded Gran as one of my first and best teachers, not only in the ways of faith but also on the contemplative path within it.

I spent many, many hours listening to her stories and imbibing her teaching (though she would never have called it that; she simply taught by her very being, as all good elders do). Faith for her was as natural as breathing, and indeed if you listened as closely as I often did to her whistled breathing as she went about her day, a short prayer to the Sacred Heart or to Our Lady was often just beneath the surface of her breath.

Like her own mother and grandmother before her,

she was a 'sharp woman', as they used to say in Dublin, meaning a wise person and one with a direct line to the spiritual world. Her mother was sought out among the Dublin flats as she had 'the way' of helping difficult births and deaths and was often asked for advice about a 'match' between couples as she had a 'good eye' for these things.

Gran was no different, and there were many times I would go over to her house to find her sitting beside the phone waiting for the call that would tell her so and so had died. She, of course, already knew as she had 'the dream' the previous night ... the phone call always came to confirm it and I soon learned to be used to it.

On other occasions, I would arrive to hear her chatting aloud with someone, only to discover her alone by the fire when I entered the room.

I never asked.

She never said.

We didn't need to.

She taught me those ways too. 'Look into the fire and tell me what you see,' she would say, and then smile when, to my surprise, I saw. She taught me to look at people's eyes when they spoke and at the way they stood and moved.

She had tremendous devotion to the Blessed Virgin, who had 'been through it all', and her prayers to her were not so much novenas or devotions as a constant conversation born of a life-long trust. She had great respect for the friars and religious orders, much preferring their churches in town where she could attend anonymously, not liking the 'front-seat parish people', as she called them.

She reminded me often never to judge anyone and taught me to give to the poor, especially beggars in the street. 'There's always a story there,' she would say. 'No one is on the street because they want to be.' Women were on the street or poor, she said, because 'men put them there'. Men were on the street or poor because 'most men are fools for the bottle or for a story'. No matter the reason, they were to be listened to and helped.

She had been sharp in other ways too. A hard life and losing her husband early on had made her hard in her midlife and it was only as a gran that she softened again. In her later years, she would often tell me that she was glad she got to be a gran after everything she had been through.

She often worried about her death, though she was not afraid to die. 'No one dies alone,' she would say. She had seen enough deaths to know that 'they come to collect you'.

She was, however, afraid that she would die in the house and that I or another grandchild would find her. So for the last few years of her life she prayed every day the 'Thirty Days Prayer' to Our Lady for a happy death, and she listed the way she wanted to go: she wanted to die in her sleep so she could 'wake up in heaven'. She wanted to die alone but having said her goodbyes and surrounded by love. She wanted to be ready to go.

She talked about it often, not in a morbid way, but in the way you recite your shopping list. Going and coming were natural in their very essence, and death, she had long taught and lived, was nothing to be afraid of for a Christian soul.

In the weeks before the Christmas she died, she had been very unwell. Pneumonia had followed a chest and kidney infection and a stay in hospital was called for. She did not want to go but acquiesced at my mum's request. Feeling a little better after a few days of antibiotics, she was to be released for Christmas by the doctors even though Mum was not sure that she was ready. She came home to us. She was weak and a slim figure of her former self, though I still wondered at the muscled arms of her small frame, a result of countless years of housework when that was a far more physical ordeal. She spent most of the next couple of days in bed, sleeping. She smiled a lot and we got to visit with her and hold her hand and chat.

Christmas Eve came and her children and grandchildren all visited with presents and smiles and the occasional worried whispered conversation with my mum and dad as to how she was doing. Christmas Day she was very quiet and slept a lot. As the house was beginning to settle down, she called my mum into the room and, very deliberately – and unusually for a woman of her time – thanked her for all she had done and told her she loved her. My mum was somewhat taken aback but, at that moment, Gran asked her who it was that was standing behind her. There was no one there that Mum could see. Gran's eyes focused on the spot behind her and she relaxed.

'It's all right,' she said, 'I know them.'

Mum said her smile was a beautiful thing at that moment.

She told Mum, 'You can go down to the family now, I'm fine.'

Mum did, though to the end of her own days she often wondered why she did. As she went downstairs, she could hear Gran talking quietly in the room.

Later, Mum checked in on her to find her sleeping deeply and gently. That night a blackbird sang outside the house all night. I remember looking out to try and see it.

I could not. I should have known.

Gran had often taught me to watch out for blackbirds. 'They are special to our family,' she would say. 'Your grandfather loved them and they come to warn us of things. Whenever you see one, say a prayer to your grandad.'

I still do.

The following morning, very early, Mum woke suddenly and went straight to check on her. Gran had passed away. She was still warm and she was smiling gently.

Mum called for the priest and the doctor and then carefully woke us all. I still remember that there were no tears in the house that morning. It all felt very peaceful and quiet. The priest administered the last rites as he felt that she had only just gone before Mum found her. A little later, myself and Mum stood in the room with Gran, we were looking out the window. On the lawn a hen blackbird was hopping around. We smiled at that.

'Well,' I said, 'she certainly got the death she wanted!'

Mum told me then about the things that had happened the previous night and about Gran seeing someone in her room. Someone who had made her smile.

'Do you think it was Grandad?' I asked.

At that moment, right in front of us, a cock blackbird, all shiny and bright-yellow-beaked, flew down beside the hen on the lawn outside. They greeted each other and flew off together.

After that, there was nothing else to say.

Gran had got the death she had asked for and we had received the little signs of her going.

In Ireland there has always been the custom of the *Cuireadh na Nollag*, the so-called 'Christmas Invitation', the feeling that a death at this time of the year is especially blessed and that the signs around it are powerful. Today, almost 30 years later, I write this so that the story of my gran's passing may be remembered and may bring peace and hope to all who read it.

And perhaps the next time you see a blackbird, you might say a prayer for all your loved ones gone before you.

St Nicholas Dawn

On the sixth morn of the month that's dark
while walking in the hallowed park,
and breathing deep the icy air
I felt the grace of Nicholas there.
I stood a moment in the frost
and felt the yearning of the lost
on land or sea, who wandering go
whose minds and hearts are often low
as gripped within by sadness grey
they stumble through another day
and long to feel the gift of light
break in upon their inner night.
Then feeling deep their dark and pain
I vowed to ne'er come there again.

Right then I felt him standing there,
all bright against the freezing air
a bishop robed in red was he,
who looked with kindness upon me.
Leaning upon his gnarled staff
his beard it shook as he did laugh,
and said in tone of deepest cheer,

'Why what on earth do we have here?
A little friar out in the cold
whose failing heart is not so bold,
for overcome with grief is he
for those whose lives in darkness be,
and those who know the belly's wail,

and those who sit alone in jail,
and those whose hearts know only pain,
and those who sleep outside in rain,
and those who fear the stronger power,
and those who nearer feel death's hour.'

And scarce he spoke, but I replied,
'Tis true you see what lies inside,
but what can I do next to you
who dwell above the azure blue,
and, as a saint, may do so much
to bring the light and healing touch
of heaven's blessing, earthward sent
to those whose lives by pain are rent?'

At this, his face, it darkened then,
as though despairing of all men,
like me who seek a grace to flow,
but far too often still say no
when called to be a mirror through,
the poor, the lame, the sickened too,
will see a glimpse of heaven's light
that lifts them from the pit of night.

Then as I stood before his face,
he touched my heart and blessed this place
and said, 'It's right that this you know,
that saint I am, and saint I go
throughout the world, both night and day
to hear the cries of those who pray,
and then I bring their yearning strong

to him who seeks to right their wrong;
then sent am I by his right hand
to all the hearts within the land
who gentled are by graces dear
and shed their sweet impassioned tear,
that they would know their call is this,
to enter into heaven's bliss
by healing, helping, lifting, raising,
listening, watching, minding, saving
the weak, the poor, the little child,
as I did here before I died.

'For this they call me Santa Claus!
I who kept sweet heaven's laws,
and now I pass them on to you,
O little one, who now dares to
extend a hand that helps and heals,
and so the light of God reveals,
to let each poor one deeply know
that Christ their saviour bowed so low
that babe he was in frost and cold,
our shepherd king who serves the fold
and in his mother's arms did cry
for all the sheep, for you and I,
and none he lost, and none forgot,
not even those who choose the lot
of greed and pride and selfish gain,
for them he offered every pain.

'So, come my friend and stand with me
beneath the branches of this tree

and we shall watch the dawn arise
and light grow in the eastern skies
and pray and psalm and praise again
the one who is the light of men.'
At this the old man smiled at me,
as we stood 'neath the ancient tree
and in my heart again I vowed
to cry to all with voice aloud,
of him who loves us deep and well,
to be a Christmas tolling bell,
that rings and calls both one and all
to heed the ancient Yuletide call,
to light each other's gathering dark
and share within the healing spark
that he first kindled with his breath,
that one who broke the power of death.

And as the light grew all around
I seemed to hear a merry sound
of bells and chimes from out the air
of laughter deep that saints do share,
and gone he was, my bishop bright,
there at the dawning of the light,
and I was left once more alone
filled with a song of heaven's tone
that flames within my heart so bright
I fear not now no lack of light.
So forth I went to sing this lay
of the light that shone on Nicholas's day.

Week One

Still Point

Slow Down Your Walk

Today, let the ancient call of Advent remind you to slow your walk. To slow down your walk until you begin to hear the song of all creation. This is the song that the cosmos has sung from the first moment of its being. This is the song your heart sings with each breath, though you know it not. Slow down, walk gently, breathe deeply and then you will bring peace and joy with you wherever you go.

Sacred Pause

How do I walk? Is it all about the destination or do I allow my gaze to seek beauty and to bring peace as I go?

Daily Meditation

Breathing in: I take a step and invite Divine Presence (come, O Lord).

Breathing out: I choose to travel in peace and quiet.

Repeat this cycle during your meditation practice. If you become distracted, just gently return to the breath without any negative judgement or agitation.

Advent Vespers

At the thinnest time of the year,
when the worlds whisper
to each other across the cosmos
and tell their ancient tales
while the darkness draws in,
we draw the cloak of comfort
close against the cold.
And, at our vesper vigilling,
a spark is struck
and enfolded
in the ever-green,
that circle of
hoped-for spring,
sprinkled with blood-berried scarlet,
of wounds wilding,
and see time's yearning path
retold in leaves,
the slow greening
of patriarch's prayer
and prophet's longing.
So we wreathe ourselves
in hope, again,
as a wavering flame
proclaims faith's abiding presence
beyond dark's doubting
and invokes the coming
of the one who is always present;
knowing that
as flame will beget flame

until the candled constellation
is complete
and our carolled voices rise
to join the sister stars
in their long remembering
of that ancient night
when, once, they
stilled their dance
awhile, and, awestruck,
watched the silent word
appear, whose light,
now hidden 'neath Mary's mantle
and settled on straw,
first kindled their flame
and set the measure
of their orbit's pace.
But in this moment's breathing
we simply stand
and psalm our way
to Advent's gates of longing,
and there, with open hands
and hearts made poor again,
we are gentled
by a single flame's appearing,
and watch soul's inward sky
for grace's first falling flake,
as children long for snow.

Our Lady of Advent

O Lady of the first Advent,
bright ray of violet dawn
glimpsed upon horizon's edge,
you promise of patriarch's prayers
and prophet's deep dreaming,
presaged by ark and veil and temple,
we call you now,
come and make us ready!
O green bud who heals the root
of the world's tree, you appear
as seed of spring in the midst
of deep sin-wintered darkness;
a light, a tindered spark,
arising from the dry-long-fruitless
wood now tender touched at last
consumed by fire,
but unburned and unburied,
appearing in the mind's eye
of all who long for light
and feel the past ages of
our benighted vision's yearning.
O bright woman, born of the long line
of Eve, hidden and hoped for
in their tears and broken hearts
and in their courage that quakes
the ages of men.
You step a girl into this world
as wisdom and benediction both,
who will draw down from heaven's halls

the promised peace,
who shatters the walls and
gates of the warmonger
and in the grace of emptiness
wakes our world soul
with hope at last
of Eden's long-lost promise
while magnifying the mystery of love.
We call you!
Come and make us ready!
O Lady of the second Advent,
you will come sky-mantled and star-crowned,
wrapped in sun splendour and moon's
slow silver stepping,
become again the great
cosmic solstice of the end,
when the dance shall cease at last
the sky shall tear and you the holy ark
be seen in the blue heaven's angeled embrace.
O come!
Make us ready for that day
when you as queen and mother
and wisdom's spouse all
open the treasure houses of the heavens,
when mercy is poured out
at your prayer and
we shall know ourselves
your sainted subjects.
We call you!
Come and make us ready!
O Lady of this Advent's present blessing,

seen in sign and circle
down the spiral of the long years appearing,
present in pillared candle flame,
green and berried branch
and open wreath's enfolding emptiness;
make of us a manger, for we are straw,
our cave hearts long for light
though the mind's inn, so filled with noise,
crowded with distracted din,
has too often no room for your birthing rest,
your saving stillness, your broken heart
by which you bear us all anew in blessing.
Come now and enter our darkness
O wise Virgin,
O green new shoot,
O wisdom wild and dangerous,
O queen, O woman,
O Lady of Advent,
we call you!
O come and make us ready.

Week Two

Still Point

Holy Solitude

Solitude
is not
empty
but
empties us
of
the
false fullness
of
the chattering mind.
It opens
us
to
the sound
behind
and
before
silence,

from which
all sounds
emerge;
the Divine Word,
from whom all that
is,
arises.
In whom all that
is,
is.
To whom all that
is,
returns:

Solitude
is not
absence,
but
embraces us
with presence.
Weaving back
our
frayed ends
into
the web
of
Divine design
it restores
our unity
within
and

without.
Gentling our
spirit and
our
speech,
yielding
us into
listening love,
until we
can
hear again
the song of praise
for
creation's
first
Divine in-breathing.
Sung now
in
an
infinitude
of voices,
each in their
own tongue,
whether
in the
ancient dialect
of
still stone
or slow sky
or tall tree
or breathing bird

or small
and
single
cell.
For,
the gift of separation
is to
heart hear
them
exult
in
elemental
excelsis
of
earth,
air,
water,
fire,
blended by
Divine blessing
into being
and fired
into
beginning – beauty
by resurrection
light.

So,
stepping into,
holy solitude
we,

emptied and
embraced,
behold
anew,
and
with joy,
as
brother
or sister,
our
graced invitation
back into
our
familial
home
of both
being,
and
blessing
when
we still
enough
to rejoin
the dance
of
Divine Love.

Daily Meditation

Breathing in: I choose to rest my heart in this moment of awareness.

Breathing out: Smiling, I journey on in love.

Repeat this cycle during your meditation practice. If you become distracted, just gently return to the breath without any negative judgement or agitation.

First Frost

First frost
last night.
Today,
in brittle sunshine,
Sunday steals in slowly,
as a robin ticks
in the cloister garden,
another mendicant amongst
the begging brothers,
waiting for breakfast crumbs.
He
invites me out
into the cold bright air
and the new beginning
that every Sunday
offers
at the altar
of heavenly bread,
where we,
the robins of the road,
brown and often
with ruffled feathers
and
hearts reddened
by his fire,
sing
and are
fed.

Week Three

Still Point

Icons – Doorways to Divine Presence

The placing of icons and sacred images around friaries, convents and monasteries is nothing to do with decoration and everything to do with sacred mindfulness.

Each image is a window into the Divine reality that enfolds every space and from which each moment arises. They are reminders, touchstones of Divine Love's presence and compassion reaching out to us in time through the lives of the holy ones.

These sacred images are meant to allow us to pause and rest, even if only for a moment on our daily journey and so begin again, having refreshed our hearts. They train us to begin to see both time and space themselves as holy so that we may eventually become able to see all that is as holy, all that is as signposts to the one who *is* love.

What are the sacred 'icons' and images in your home that elicit this response? They may be as simple as family photos and souvenirs of travel, or as deliberately sacred as a dedicated home altar or meditation space.

Whether you pause before icons or even simply in front of nature itself, may your pause become prayer and your prayer become peace.

Sacred Pause

What images around my home and work allow moments of resting in Divine Presence? What would it look like to have points of spiritual refreshment in all that I look at during the day?

Daily Meditation

Breathing in: I am aware that I am called to be an icon of Divine Presence.

Breathing out: I gaze at a sacred image and hear its call to wake to presence.

Repeat this cycle during your meditation practice. If you become distracted, just gently return to the breath without any negative judgement or agitation.

Angels Overhead

Angels are always everywhere,
for those with eyes to see.
Bestowing benediction, they
mediate meaningful meetings,
and make miracles for sacred citizens
of seemingly secular cities
who, unaware, unknowing, unknown,
and feeling franticly fearful, forget
to stop still,
pause peacefully and
luminously look up
from daily duty's drive
so as to
glance at grace's gifts
falling freely and as
slow as snowflakes
upon beetled brows;
where they
release rest
in heavy-hearted humans
who, despite dark deeds,
from which freed and forgiven,
will co-create kingdom
by child's new choosing
of wild wonder.

Traditionally in Europe, 16 December marked the feast of the greening, when evergreen branches were brought to the churches and monasteries to decorate the sanctuaries and prepare them for Christmas. This would eventually become conflated with the custom of the Christmas tree in our homes.

The Greening

December,
and the Cold Moon
wanes tonight,
sharp-edged as ice,
like a peephole cut
in the night sky,
she looks into
a realm of pure light,
casting her long shadows
across the frosted glass ground
scribbled by bare black branches.
Above the diamond-lit stars,
below the glittering snows,
reminders both that even
the darkest of winter days
gives way at last to dawn.
Now the night of greening comes
as in defiance of the cold and dark
the forest is foraged for the gift of life
hidden in its grey sleeping hills.
Comes forth the ivy,

in her tenacity and strength!
Comes forth the holly,
bright-berried and blood-blessed!
Comes forth the red rowan,
long mountain born!
Comes forth the fir tree,
in her verdant mantle!
Now nature once again
hallows the halls
of consecrated stone,
illuminating the cloisters
and the Advent-purpled apse
as scribes once warmed
the word with colour.
Leaf and branch and winter fruit
gathered and laid as offerings
bringing life and warmth
into the place of peace,
clothing the Advent wreath
and its singing people
in circling sanctuary!
Lighting our longing
we lay them for
our saviour evergreen
who brought forth
the new spring
in the libation of his bright blood
upon the old earth,
in the Divine seed planted
upon the rocky skull,
there overcoming the old

sin-wintered death's stroke at our roots,
he grafts us to himself anew
our Advent Adam, binding the knot
in swaddling, and breathing
new blessing over the earth,
as with his holy birth
a breeze from summerlands
hits hard and drives back
the cold and dark!
He the true source of our verdant life,
a root renewed,
a shoot green and bursting,
born from a thornless rose
that blooms this winter night,
blessed beneath the whitest snow,
as now the greening comes again.

Week Four

Still Point

Christmas Eve – Lighting the Lamp of Welcome

Irish tradition says that the holy family still travel
throughout the world this night seeking shelter.
Is there room for them at your inn?
Is there room for them at my inn?
Can you see them pass by?
Joseph lost in thought,
Mary tired and heavy with child.
Can you see their eyes looking out at you from the eyes of
the homeless, the poor,
the excluded, the refugee, the immigrant,
the elderly, the child, the lonely,
the victim of war, the abused, the hungry, the persecuted,
the one you have already judged,
the one I have already judged?
If you would recognise them
then slow down,
let your hands unclench,
simply breathe,

and light a candle
of welcome in the
window of your soul.
As the old poem put it:
'Often, often, often
goes the Christ
in the stranger's guise'.

Sacred Pause

The old customs of cleaning the house and lighting a lamp of welcome for the holy family on Christmas Eve can become new and meaningful once again if we approach them mindfully and with contemplative awareness. Who do we need to welcome, to remember, to invite in order to truly live the Christmas message in our own hearts and lives today?

Daily Meditation

Breathing in: I welcome this sacred moment of Christmas.

Breathing out: I welcome all the parts of me that need to come home to light.

Repeat this cycle during your meditation practice. If you become distracted, just gently return to the breath without any negative judgement or agitation.

The Coming of Christmas

We have candled your coming
O Lord of love.
As from the deep dark
we have watched and waited
your wombing into world;
lit lamps of longing
in our Advent art
and found freedom in
ancient avenues,
tread tirelessly,
by generation's genius
of seeing in simple cycles
the birth of new beginnings,
as, through years' yearnings
and pasts now present
in eternal echoes.
We have heard our
heart's hunger
for mystic meaning
and so, as stars stop
and become still,
we feel soul's sounding
of innocence's invasion;
the incarnation.
Heavenly healing of
sin-sundered souls
through Mary's mothering
'Yes' and yielding
to Divine decisions' descent

until the ultimate
transcends time
and we are woken
at midnight's moment
by babe's first breath;
inward inspiration of straw
and dung-warmed air,
that fuels the first wail of the Word
whose kingdom comes
in earth's embrace and
mother's mantle
to offer us love's light.

A Meditation for Christmas Eve, Eve

Shhh.
Come away a moment,
my friend.
Come away
from the lights,
and the crowds,
and the shops,
and the noise,
and the pressure,
and the worries,
and the old wounds that
winter us
before our time.
Come and sit with me here.
Rest.
Just for a moment.
Let me share with you once again
what we forget in our festive
frenzy:
he is coming ...
Down the long ages of despair
he comes as hope.
Down the rough road of doubt
he comes as faith.
Down the broken byways
of the
human heart
he comes as love.
He is coming ...

Sit with me on the edge of waiting ...
Sit in sacred stillness ...
Breathe the deep breath of
blessing.
You do not have to do anything.
He is coming ...
Whether you are ready or not
aware or not,
able or not,
present or not,
believing or not,
he is coming ...
As the sun rises,
as the moon shines,
as the tides turn,
as the stars dance,
he is coming ...
So do not worry.
Let the tyranny of
tension
fall from you ...
You never needed to carry it.
Let the false face of
righteous readiness to defend,
dissolve.
You never needed to wear it.
How could you ever be ready
for this?
For the first proclamation of the
kingdom to be heard in a baby's
cry.

Nothing is asked of you
but
to be here and now,
who you are.
Truly.
Fully.
Broken?
Yes.
Weak?
Yes.
Called?
Oh yes.
He is coming …
And he is calling you to come to him.
As he always does.
As he always will.
So, how will you greet him,
the one who is coming?
The one who calls you,
to his crib.
(Yes, you.)
Will you prepare a place for him?
Will you open the cave of your heart to him?
Will you place him in the sanctuary of your soul?
Will you lay him upon the rough straw of your life?
Will you swaddle him with your silence?
Will you offer him the gentle warmth of animal breath?
Will you offer him your love?
Or not.
He is coming …
Do not miss the moment

of mystery's
mangered birth
by succumbing to
Bethlehem busyness.
No.
Become as still as a shepherd watching the flock of
slumbering sheep.
Become as still as a sage watching the long dance
of the stars.
Become as still as Joseph hearing angels on the
edge of dreams.
Become as still as she who is the stillpoint of love's
longing, filled with light.
Be still and you will know
he is coming ...
Always ...
In stillness,
on the edge of waiting ...
He is coming for you ...
He is coming to you ...
Always.
He is coming in love.

Christmas Eve Dawn

Full moon
leads to first frost
a silvered start to the day
breath catching
beauty outlined
in sharp filigree of wonder.
A clarity in the air
that child's tired sight
and weary heart both
arresting in its very sharpness
it gives the soft curves
of leaf and land
an edge that beckons beyond
to the place where once again
we become aware
of every breath
as gift, as birth,
as blessing,
seeing now our singing
made visible before us
hang in the cold
carolling
the welcome
to the Word
made flesh
in frosted
time.

The Wild Nativity

We have our prophecies too, you know.
We tell our own tales,
and so we knew to gather there that night,
ambassadors of our varied kinds all.
Before old Joseph came back with supplies from the inn.
We were there.
Hidden in the hay.
Or up amongst the old beams.
Or resting by the manger.
Or drawn there by the new star
that rose that night, pure and shining
like a snowflake in its light.
We were there.
We had felt the old pull of Eden
in our furred and feathered hearts,
and felt his long-remembered nearness
once again, who walked with us too in evening light.
Old rivalries forgotten, or at least put aside tonight,
we sat peacefully in storied rank half hidden in the shadows,
lost in awe at her,
settled so still in the straw,
her eyes closed,
as though present to a mystery within.
We were there.
Waiting for him, with her.
Let us prepare
his place, we said.
Wren moved first,
to pluck her own breast
scattering the softest down

amongst the rough straw.
Sparrows followed
weaving moss and herbs
as mattress
as owl, and old crow
and even sharp-eyed hawk directed.
'I will keep him warm,'
said robin, reddening his breast
while fanning flame alight.
'We will sing to him
when at last he comes,'
said the little ones,
four-footed and furred,
short- and long-tailed too,
piping in their tiny voices
choiring high, as mouse
and vole, rabbit
and hedgehog all
assembled there,
followed by fox's clear tenor
and badger's earthy baritone
to sing their benediction of
wild welcome.
And then, he came.
How?
As sun shines sudden through a cloud,
breaking blindingly!
How?
As the first rays of dawn mark that moment
when night becomes a new day.
How?

As a scenting nose is suddenly aware
of a change in the air.
He came.
More than that, we will not say.
Ours alone was that privilege to see and we will guard it
down the ages.
And Mary looked upon us with love
and thanked us all
as in her smile and words
we heard old Eve laugh
at last again.
And then there was noise,
and people, so many people!

And we withdrew
as we always do
to the shadows again.
But not before he smiled at us
a smile of long recognition
graced and grateful both.
After the shepherds left,
and their piping drumming din
went off amongst the crowds.
After Bethlehem finally became still.
After old Joseph nodded off
to his angeled dreams.
We were there.
We came forth again
from the shadows
to dwell with them,
our new Adam and Eve,
and heard then our secret gospel

preached to us, who are already
of his kingdom and always were.
We made our covenant
with him then,
to be the first apostles of his love
and in our being, blessed
and shared with you
to remind you of the innocence
you once lost and he renews
if you would but follow
our wild way to Eden's light again.
We have been forgotten now
as shepherds, kings
and crowds followed,
but not by him,
who from his mother's arms
smiled past them all at us
hiding in the shadows there.
We would later meet him
in the desert and the garden,
there we would be with him again,
for we have our prophecies too,
you know.
We tell our tales too,
whispering to each other
across the woods and hills,
on this night each year.
As you toll your bells and sing,
we look to the skies
and remember:
we were there.

Wintry

A dreary day, you say?
Wintry yes, but dreary?
There I choose to differ.
Remember.
What have you seen along the way?
The winter cherries are beginning to bloom
in the gardens along the road.
Small flurries of blossom erupt from frosted buds
launching clouds of colour skywards.
Pink, white and delicate as castor sugar dusting they
soften sight like unlooked-for blessings.
Yes, the red, gold and purple leaves have all fallen, but
now their breeze-shifting shapes make a kaleidoscope of
the forest floor,
while overhead the bare branches describe their
complicated winter geometry to the wind, each twig an
ink stick scribbling on the sky.
Along the street the lamps are early lit
in windows and paint the pavement yellow, gold and orange,
shining boxes of warmth and light, out and upward into
early darkness;
behind each a mind, a soul, a heart on fire with all the
subtle colours of emotions' ever-shifting palette painting
stories of days' doings in their words.
Christmas trees and silvered lights make of the land a
mirror to our constellated sky,
each a drop of glimmer grace, each a bell calling us to
home and hearth and beyond again at last to Bethlehem.
Look up, my friend.

Look around, about and then within,
You daily live a rainbowed life,
so praise this winter dark, a blessed yearly
chance to see again the light, the colours that
shine beneath, behind all things
from which the light arises
out of which the colour comes.

Old Crow

Old crow in the snow
Sits upon the bough
Old crow in the snow
Only thinks of now
Winter comes
And winter goes
And soon will come again
For passing fast
Are the lives
Of fragile little men
So in the snow
The old crow
Watches from the height
Not for him their to and fro
But only seeking light
With his caw
Will come the thaw
Then spring will fill the lands
And green and bright
Will be the trees
And warm will be my hands
Then bough will break
And he will take
To flight and soar away
Until the cold
Returns to hold
Again its frozen sway.
But for now
Upon the bough

Sits the ancient crow
All robed in black
He feels no lack
But only falling snow
So I must be
Just like he
And put my thoughts away
That long for when
And yearn for then
But never settled lay
So be instead
By old crow led
Who sits upon the bough
And feel the snow
Upon my head
And only think of now

The gift of the animal world to us is that they show us what it is like to exist almost exclusively in the present moment.

Wonder

Sometimes, the sheer
is-ness of it all
threatens to overwhelm me
with wonder.
The way the light,
falling over the cup or the chair
pours itself in such a way
as to reveal its inner life,
its gift of existence,
its combination of atom
and element and age,
with intention and insight and art,
to simply become the cup,
or the chair.
To say nothing
of the infinitude
of mystery that is
tree, or cat, or rock,
or bird, or,
above all, the you
that is reading this,
the I that is writing it,
attempting
to capture meaning
and pass on mystery
by marks upon a page
from my mind to yours,
from my heart to yours,
so that in that moment
of mutual awareness

we are in some small way
one in the words.
Sometimes the sheer
almost not-ness
of it all
threatens to overwhelm me
with wonder.
The way so many circumstances
must come together to produce
the chair or the cup,
so that its raw
elemental being
could have
been conjured,
brought to birth,
from essence to form,
travelling through
the infinitude of idea,
from imaginal
to extant.
To say nothing
of the immensity
of mysterious conditions
which, over aeons,
led down the ages
to that creation
we call tree, we call cat,
we call rock, we call bird,
or that one we call
you.
How many generations

did it take for you to be?
How many
meetings of hearts?
How many
circumstances of life?
How many
precise moments?
How many steps
that were
just so?
So that now
you and I
may be,
here, and now,
dancing through
the field of Divine
possibility,
wherein the eternal
is-ness
calls out our being
from the infinitude of
not-ness.
Come consider
all that is.
Come consider
your being.
Come be
overwhelmed
just a little every day
by the wonder
of it all,

by the oneness
of our diversity,
as we are called forth,
as we are re-minded
of the mystery,
as we touch with
awareness
that you, and I,
and all that is,
though always
almost not,
through love's longing,
are.

New Year's Eve

What of last year?
Be not afraid
to let it go.
All of it;
the joys and the sorrows,
the burdens and the blessings.
Put them down gently and,
with reverence, place them
into the wounded hands
of Divine mercy
and then receive back from
the source of all love
the only real gift
that you may bring into
the new year; wisdom.
What of the new year?
Be not afraid ...
but enter it with joy.
Welcome all of the gifts
it waits to bestow,
knowing that,
when you rest secure
in the infinite love
that dwells in the wounded heart
of Divine mercy,
then all becomes grace;
the joys and the sorrows,
the burdens and the blessings,
and you will receive back

from the source of all love
the only real gift
that any year can bring:
wisdom.
Tonight, however you choose to spend it,
alone or with others,
in quiet introspection
or in loud celebration,
in the moment between last year
and new year,
breathe deep, pause,
and know that in places
all over the world
you are being held in prayer
and blessed in your new beginning.

From Lent to Easter:
An Annual Retreat

Lent: The Season of the Desert

Ash Wednesday is the first day of the holy season of the Great Lent. The ashes we bless and wear on this day signify our common humanity, our union with Mother Earth and the deep healing we need from God for the wounds our sins have caused in ourselves and others; healing that is already ours in Christ Jesus. To awaken us more fully to these realities we take these 40 days of prayer, fasting and almsgiving as 'spiritual bootcamp' to prepare for the feast of Easter.

Whatever you do extra or give up for Lent, do it with love and with the intention that your heart opens ever more fully to the healing and compassion of God. If entered with awareness, then the 40 days of Lent can be a wonderful annual retreat that brings us more deeply into the presence of Divine Love.

Traditionally, Lent is a season of increased prayer, fasting and almsgiving. These ancient remedies deepen our sensitivity to the movement of the Holy Spirit in our lives and bring about a deep inner turning towards the true meaning of human life, communion with God and with one another that brings about the building of the kingdom, the reign of God in our souls.

We begin the season with the imposition of ashes upon the forehead, one of the oldest scriptural signs of someone turning their life towards Divine Love and away from selfishness and egoism. We begin by reflecting upon this sacred sign.

Week One of Lent

Still Point

Ash Wednesday

And so Lent begins
with holy ash ...
A reminder of the dust we come from, breathed into life
by love ...
A reminder of the ashes of our past, the sins and the
burdens we are exhausted from carrying ...
A reminder of the desert spaces where life has not been
allowed to enter ...
A reminder of the dark spaces that shut out the light ...
A reminder of our bodily destiny, our dissembling into
dust again when our last breath will breathe its way back
to love ...
We bear the holy ash today, not proudly, but as the mark
of one who knows their need for the renewing breath
of the one who *is* love, is life, is light – the one who will
call us into the desert of transformation, the desert of
conversion, the desert of the cross and there sow seeds
of resurrection joy that will bloom from the ashen

dust, irrigated by tears of truth, warmed by the sun of love, made fertile by the planting of prayer within its barrenness.

So Lent begins and together we each enter its desert to be alone with him who makes the desert bloom again.

Blessings on you and yours this Lenten season.

Week Two of Lent

Still Point

Transfiguration

With the second Sunday of Lent we meditate upon the transfiguration of the Lord. Traditionally, the story of Jesus ascending the mountain and there revealing his divinity to his closest disciples was often used to test the awareness of novice meditators who were asked by their masters the old question: 'On the mountain who changed?'

While after a cursory glance at the story many would reply incorrectly that 'Jesus changed on the mountain', those who had gone a little deeper in their practice would see that it was the disciples who changed as they saw Jesus as he truly is, not just on the mountain, but always.

This deep, contemplative reading of the scripture allows us to recognise that as we progress in our meditative practice we begin to see reality as it actually is, transfigured always by Divine Love and a gateway always to Divine presence.

Week Three of Lent

Still Point

Living from the Heart

On the Fridays of Lent we meditate on the mystery of the cross of Christ as the revelation of God's infinite love and mercy. At the centre of the cross, we find the heart.

In Christian (and Jewish) spirituality the noetic centre – the centre and totality of all you are as an individual, as a person, the centre of your soul – is referred to as the 'heart'.

It is the heart that loves, forgives, wills and contemplates, and this centre of life, personhood and love is often identified in the physical body with the heart organ and so the journey of the spiritual life was often spoken of as the journey of the mind into the heart, there to find the presence of God dwelling at its centre.

At the centre of the cross, we find a heart. But not just any heart … we find the Sacred Heart of Jesus. A human heart, yes, a heart that existed in time, that was formed in the womb of his mother and there began to beat, a heart that pumped life's blood and a heart that felt all of the strains of human life until the last breath, the breath upon the cross, a breath of love freely surrendered to the Father.

A heart that after death was pierced through and that poured out on the world the twin streams of blood and water, of mercy and grace. The two streams that, to this day, pour into the world constantly through the church. A heart that lay wounded, cold and still in the grave for three days until Easter dawn.

Our God has a heart – a human heart that knows our weakness and our pain, even the pain of death.

Our God has a heart – a Sacred Heart filled with infinite love and mercy for each of us.

His risen heart beats with love for you, is on fire with love for you.

At the centre of the cross, we find the Christ.

At the centre of the Christ, we find the heart.

At the centre of our own heart, we find his Sacred Heart, dwelling within us and holding us in being through love.

Week Four of Lent

Still Point

Cleansing the Inner Eye

All of our Lenten discipline – our prayer, our fasting, our almsgiving – amounts simply to this:

- to allow the pure water of grace to cleanse the eye of awareness of all distraction from Divine Light;
- to allow the embrace of holy desire to awaken our hearts to Divine Love;
- to allow the healing breath of the Holy Spirit to vivify in us Divine life.

For when we allow this Divine activity, we become the place where the bearing of the cross becomes the place of resurrection for us and for all. This means not just entering into stillness in the midst of our meditation and prayer but carefully discerning what we allow 'in' through the gates of our senses.

Our Lenten asceticism is not just giving things up to be a little healthier physically, but a deep discernment that allows us to acknowledge what we give our inner attention to, and to decide what should be accepted and what let go in order to grow in mindful awareness of Divine Love.

Week Five of Lent

Still Point

With Lazarus in the Tomb

In the fifth week of Lent, we traditionally meditate on the story of Lazarus, the friend of Jesus who was raised from the dead by Christ four days after he had died. In the story, Jesus seems to delay on purpose when he is first asked to come and heal his ailing friend. However, his delay will allow the glory of Divine Love and presence to be seen by his disciples.

In the contemplative tradition, this scripture is often meditated upon during times of apparent deadness in our practice, when God seems to be distant or even non-existent. The meditator knows that this experience is necessary as a purification of our intention and for the strengthening of our practice beyond simple feel-good experiences. The tomb of Lazarus is a place of quiet faith abiding even past apparent death, a cocooning in the knowing that, once invited, Christ will always come and will always come at the best time.

Week Six of Lent

Still Point

Palm Sunday

Holy Week begins with Palm Sunday, a time to reflect on the extremes within us.

The same crowd who greet Jesus as king and Lord and sing 'Hosanna!' will shout 'Crucify him!' barely a week later. It is a reminder to us all of the potential for both good and evil present within our hearts: just because we are crying out 'Hosanna' in this moment does not mean that we may not fall and find ourselves crucifying him in the next.

Palm Sunday in its two gospel passages sobers us, and gives us a vision of human reality, our reality. Beginning in joy and ending in sorrow, it reminds us what happens when we try and shrink God, when we try and manipulate him into what we want him to be – or, even worse, into what we want him to want us to be.

The crowds shouting 'Hosanna' do exactly this. They are good people, God-fearing people even, and that may be their problem; they fear but they do not love. Love expands our understanding, fear shrinks it. In their fear and anger, their understanding is limited and so they want God to submit to them, to follow their plan. They want Jesus to be their conquering messiah, a warlord who raises an army and frees the chosen people from their Roman overlords. They don't want what God wants to give: not a warlord messiah but a suffering servant who frees, not just a city or a people from physical domination and slavery, but the whole cosmos from the slavery of sin and evil. They do not want it, but they receive not a king upon a throne, but a lamb upon a cross.

And so 'Hosanna!' can turn to 'Crucify!' so easily, so quickly. It can do that in my heart, in your heart too. Anytime we try and shrink or constrain God to our plans, our way of thinking, or our agendas, no matter how worthy or good they seem to be, this is what happens.

So what is our way out of this mess? Jesus shows us. In all of the chaos of palms and processions, he is simply himself: silent, still, present. He submits to the will of the Father and empties himself so that we may be filled. In the house of the high priest, before Pilate and even on the cross, he is simply following the will of the Father and so is serene, secure, still. He is the still point of pure love around which the world, the cosmos, turns, and, in his stillness he opens for us an ever-expanding vision of God, an ever-expanding vision of love.

Holy (Maundy) Thursday: The Day of the Gifts of Presence

As sister moon rises this evening, the Easter triduum begins ... the three days that are 'one great day', one continuous action of Divine Love.

We begin with the day of the gifts ...

Three parting gifts are given by the Lord to his followers today and each of them is usually celebrated in our evening mass of the Lord's supper. Each of them is a way of meeting the Lord's real presence, and each is a sign of love and a transforming grace that, when met, changes the person and invites them into a deeper communion of love with God in the other person.

What are these gifts we celebrate today?

They are the gift of the *holy eucharist*, the gift of the *sacramental priesthood* and the gift of the *new commandment of love (mandatum novum)*, from which the day, Maundy Thursday, takes its name.

In the commandment of love, the old law is fulfilled, completed and superseded and the operating philosophy, theology and methodology of the church is given. Our God is the one who bows low and serves his people; loving them back into wholeness. The example he gives, we are to follow. We have no part with Christ if we do not bow low too and find the Divine Presence in each other. In the taking off of the outer garment, he removes all that would separate us from himself; in the wearing of the apron, he becomes the servant and the lamb; in the washing of the feet, he prepares us for the journey into the depths of love.

In the sacramental priesthood, he establishes an eternal conduit of sacrificial grace in which the eternal salvific events about to unfold may be touched in time by each succeeding generation. In the emptying of self that the priest is called to, especially in the sacramental moment, he is present and his people touch his power and love and mercy. His priesthood is a servant, sacrificial priesthood, and his priests are called to follow the lamb to the altar and to calvary.

In the holy eucharist, he gives love's greatest gift; love itself remains incarnate and eternal with his people for all time. In this unspeakable and awe-inspiring gift of Divine generosity, he demonstrates the sheer immensity of Divine Love and its longing to be with, to be in communion with, us. He becomes our food, our medicine, our soul spouse, and the furnace in which we are purified and become what we were always meant to be. He does all this for us who are about to betray, run away and crucify him.

And he does it now today too, in this moment and in every succeeding moment, calling out to us from the priesthood, from the altar, from the blessed sacrament: 'A new commandment I leave unto you; that you love one another as I have loved you.'

Good Friday:
The Day of the Cross

Why the cross? Why of all the possible modes of execution was the cross chosen?

The ancient Fathers of the church list a number of reasons. Here are a few of them:

Crucifixion was reserved for the worst criminals and was considered the worst punishment. In absolute humility, Christ takes on the worst of what humanity can offer so as to raise us up to the best.

Sin and death entered the world through what hung from a tree; so it was conquered and banished by he who hung from the tree of the cross.

Christ is nailed between heaven and earth. His arms open wide in the embrace of infinite Divine Love. He restores the ancient communion between heaven and earth forever in his own death.

The vertical axis of the cross represents the eternal now of God piercing forever the horizontal axis of time, thus in the incarnation of Christ and through his passion and death we have access to the eternal loving *now* of God always. At the centre of this piercing we have the pierced heart of Christ from which flows the streams of sacramental grace that we call the church.

This is the atonement, literally the 'at-one-ment', that Christ accomplished through his death on the cross – the rebalancing and healing of the ancient wound of sin that separated humanity from God and threw the whole cosmos out of balance. Now, healed by Christ through the cross, it becomes our way home again. As Augustine says, 'He descended so that we could ascend with him.'

Wherever you are today, pause simply to consider the cross.

Holy Saturday

The Vigil in the Holy Night

We have kept vigil; we have waited with hope; we vigil with all of Christianity, with all of the cosmos who since that first Good Friday have entered into the Divine space where these sacred events always exist, at once both human and Divine, in time and in eternity.

We have walked their ancient paths, worn by countless generations of faith-filled ancestors all over the world, and we have arrived at that upper room where the disciples and apostles gather to wait. For what, they do not know, they are simply called to wait. Sustained by a silent mother in their midst who believes as only a mother can believe that the story of her broken boy is not yet over, cannot yet be over, must not yet be over. She a single, silent point of illumined faith in a world of darkness and pain, a star shining in the night dark in despair.

Let us go to that place now and be with them a while,

entering in spirit that room of darkened windows and locked doors where, since yesterday afternoon, they have descended into that quiet that enters the human heart when, hoping against hope, we wait ...

We wait...

We wait ... when waiting itself seems a vain act, a hopeless effort of a heart and mind too broken to take in the awful reality of what has just happened.

The world would call it denial, it would see in it a people who are broken by their own betrayal of the one they claimed they loved and who now cannot accept the consequences of that betrayal. And so they leave us alone; their work is done, our work is done. We betrayed him, they crucified him. No matter who did what, who held the nails, who held the scourge, who placed the crown of thorns upon his head, he is dead. That is all. And so they leave them at the tomb, leave them to crawl back to the upper room of vigilling. Of waiting ... of silence.

We look around the room ... and remember ... Can it really be only a few days since he was here, speaking, teaching, loving? We see the bowl of water, the towel, we see the empty plate and cup, we remember his call to love and we remember his prediction of betrayal and how, just for a moment, almost none of them, none of us, could meet his eyes.

We try and stop remembering ... instead we wait with them, not really sure of what we are waiting for, there is simply a silent insistence to be here ... to gather, to wait, and, sometimes, when we think no one is watching or listening, to weep, to weep for what we saw, those of us who stayed and walked behind him in the crowd; to weep for what we didn't see, those of us who fled to rooms and hills and hidden places where, though we did not see it all we felt it all, heard it all.

Sometimes, it is harder to feel and to hear than it is to see – especially when the mocking voice arises from the silence of our hearts and sneeringly delivers us to the edge of despair as we look back and watch our brave words crumble into cowardice.

And so we wait … we wait as people have always waited at sickbeds and deathbeds, at moments of birth and moments of breaking, at moments of making and unmaking. We wait with the earth our mother, and the sun and the stars our elder sisters and brothers – those powers who stopped in their tracks and hid their faces and broke open in horror at what their human brothers and sisters had done, at what we had done. We wait as armies await the dawn hoping for the cry of a new day and a new hope. And slowly, hesitatingly, we remember …

Did he not say that this would happen? Did he not speak to us of a handing over, of a death that had to be faced, of an hour that had to come. Did he not berate us for not understanding, for not believing. Did he not in this very room, only a few hours ago, tell us, as he broke the bread and blessed the cup, that he would be taken from us but that he would return … and that then he would always be with us.

We hear his words in our hearts.

At first, they are weak sounding, against the so new and so near sight of blood and nails and spear … and … blood … so much blood, poured out upon the earth. They are weak against the memory of his groans and words in the midst of agony upon the cross.

The words sound themselves in our hearts, and with each one we shudder at the remembrance:

'Father, forgive them, they know not what they do ...'

'Today you will be with me in paradise ...'

'Mother, behold your son ...'

'Son, behold your mother ...'

'My God, my God, why have you forsaken me ...?'

'I thirst ...'

'Father ... into your hands I commend my spirit ...'

And as they sound we remember that last groan, that almost silent word ... more of a breath, a gasp, fighting its way to the surface to be heard ... *'Kaaaah laaahhh'* ... 'It is accomplished'.

And somewhere deep in our memory awakens the knowing that this is the word the high priest utters in the temple as the last Passover lamb is slaughtered ... *'Kahlah'* ... 'It is accomplished'.

And we are stilled ...

and we think ...

the lamb ...

the blood of the Passover lamb ...

the blood daubed on doorpost and lintel that says in this place death has no power.

And we remember a man, John, worn thin and brown by prayer and desert sun both, and his arm, wiry and long, as it pointed across the river and his voice crying aloud, 'Behold the lamb!' And we, they, all of us through all time begin to hope, begin to yearn, begin to pray, begin to think ... maybe ... just maybe ...

For yes, he was truly the long-awaited lamb and the true high priest and even the altar of sacrifice itself, and in that whispered moan of '*Kahlah*' as he yielded up his spirit he accomplished all that he had been sent to do, all that he had freely chosen.

In emptying himself of glory, he descended into the darkness of a sin-conquered world and became its liberator, its conqueror, its saviour, its light. And we who know that darkness, who know its pull and hear its siren call daily, know also that we are made for that light, long for that light, long for that love, long in the deepest places of our hearts for new beginning and the grace of an inward dawn that never yields to the night of self or death or sin again.

And this is what we vigil for, this is how we can endure the memory of the scourge, the crown, the nails, the cross, the spear – because we know how the story ended! Not in the dark despair of a Friday night, at the sealed dry rock of a tomb, but in the dawn light of a spring garden on a Sunday morning where resurrection was announced by birds greeting the new day in song.

For in that Divine breathing forth, that cry of '*Kahlah*',
Life itself went forth to meet death,
Light itself went forth to meet darkness,
Love itself went forth to meet hate, and ...
death was made the door of life,
darkness was dispelled and illumined, and
hate was defeated and cast down by love and
breath-born creation was in-spired again;
created anew as in the saviour's expiration it
received the breath of God,
the Divine kiss of life saving a sin-drowned cosmos,
and so could begin to breathe anew.

And this happened …

this happened …

and it is happening now, here in this place …

not again, but always!

For in the eternal now of God, this waiting in the darkness of sorrow always becomes, when transcended with faith, a vigil of light and hope, always becomes a resurrection moment as we touch the power of the risen one and his grace.

And this is how by fire, and story, and water, and bread, and wine we pass through thousands of years of waiting and longing in a single night, and with hearts made new and candles kindled, we become who we really are: the anointed sons and daughters of God who know that the despair of the upper room on that Saturday will surely, surely, yield to Easter joy and light.

This is why we are able to not just tell the story but to become the story for a world that longs to hear it, needs to hear it, was made to hear it. And when we become that story in the risen one, when we allow him to, once more, be the word made flesh in us, then, only then, does the marvel of Easter take place:

Christ will rise in your heart, in my heart.

Christ will work in us and through us.

Christ will pour out his blood upon us and breathe his spirit into us and illumine us with his light and with his love.

And when the moment comes for us to enter into his kingdom, we will hear him say, as he looks upon us all, '*Kahlah!*' … 'It is accomplished!', and we will know ourselves to truly be his new creation, his victory song, his Easter people who sing his alleluia cry.

This is why we vigil and this will be why we vigil to the end of time.

Yes, we have touched darkness, and will touch it again, earthly and fallible and fallen as we are.

We have seen how quickly our 'Hosannas!' turn to cries of 'Crucify!' and we know our sin, but we know our saviour too and know that no darkness, however powerful it seems, will stand against his resurrection light.

No need for shame or guilt or fear, this holiest of nights, they are the fruits of Adam's turning away. Now the new Adam appears, and, with him who is both God and man, we are returned not merely to Eden, but to heaven itself, there to gaze upon the face of God forever and to hear our names called as children of the most high.

Yesterday we kissed the cross,

This evening we have vigilled from darkness to light

Tomorrow and forever ... we are an Easter people for we know that above all, beyond all, behind all:

Christ has died,

Christ is risen,

Christ will come again!

Easter Sunday

The Art of Resurrection

How is it possible
not to believe in resurrection;
when daily it is
accomplished around you?
When from sleep's dark and purple night
the Divine rhythm, so long laid down
pulses playing from dream
and form is freed in waking
while colour washes the sky clean
and the birds sing
their holy astonishment
at seeing the light again
for one more day.
Where were you then,
this dawning,
when the daily Easter

Exultet took place?
To what noise
were your ears tuned?
To what sights
your eyes?
Did you begin with faith
in the beauty that awaited you
beyond the door
of your snoozing senses;
or did you
soldier slumber
at the tomb
of your yesterdays
unwilling to have
your gaze lifted
to sky's summoning
to a new start?
No matter!
This miracle awaits you
every day,
with Divine patience.
Come then, and join
the dawn chorus of delight
and allow sun and sky and sea;
bird and bush and beast
to teach you the ancient
wild resurrection art
of blessed beginning.

Sacred Pause

Easter Illumination
With each cycle of in-breath and out-breath we can pray
each line deeply in our hearts or if we are by ourselves
chanting out loud.

Christ is risen! Alleluia! Alleluia!
The one who *is* light has illumined our darkness
The one who *is* life has conquered our death
The one who *is* love has transformed us into love!
Christ is risen! Alleluia! Alleluia!

The Holy Rosary

Start by making the sign of the cross:
In the name of the Father and of the Son and of the Holy
Spirit.
Amen.
Then recite the Creed:

I believe in God, the Father almighty,
Creator of heaven and earth,
and in Jesus Christ, his only Son, our Lord.
He was conceived by the Holy Spirit,
and born of the Virgin Mary.
He suffered under Pontius Pilate,
was crucified, died and was buried.
He descended into hell.
On the third day he rose again.
He ascended into heaven,
and is seated at the right hand of God the Father almighty.
He will come again to judge the living and the dead.
I believe in the Holy Spirit,
the Holy Catholic Church,
the communion of saints,
the forgiveness of sins,
the resurrection of the body,
and life everlasting.

Then say one *Our Father*, three *Hail Marys* for the virtues of faith, hope and charity; and then one *Glory Be*:

Our Father, who art in heaven, hallowed be thy name. Thy kingdom come, thy will be done, on earth as it is in heaven. Give us this day, our daily bread, and forgive us our trespasses, as we forgive those who trespass against us; and lead us not into temptation, but deliver us from evil.

Hail Mary, full of grace, the Lord is with thee. Blessed art thou among women, and blessed is the fruit of thy womb, Jesus. Holy Mary, mother of God, pray for us sinners now, and at the hour of death.

Glory Be to the Father, and to the Son, and to the Holy Spirit. As it was in the beginning, is now, and ever shall be, world without end.

The Rosary is divided into four parts, each having five mysteries. The mysteries are as follows:

Joyful
Annunciation to Mary
Visitation of Mary to Elizabeth
The Nativity of Jesus
The Presentation of Jesus in the Temple
The Finding of Jesus in the Temple

Sorrowful
The Agony of Jesus in the Garden
The Scourging of Jesus

The Crowning with Thorns
The Carrying of the Cross
The Crucifixion and Death of Jesus

Luminous
The Baptism of Jesus by John
The Miracle of Cana
The Proclamation of the Gospel
The Transfiguration of Jesus
The Institution of the Holy Eucharist

Glorious
The Resurrection of Jesus
The Ascension of Jesus
The Descent of the Holy Spirit
The Assumption of Mary into Heaven
The Crowning of Mary as Queen of Heaven

While meditating on the mysteries, recite for each
mystery:

- one *Our Father*
- ten *Hail Marys* and
- one *Glory Be*

After each mystery the 'Fatima Prayer' may be said:

O my Jesus, forgive us our sins, save us from the fires of
hell, lead all souls to heaven, especially those who are in
most need of thy mercy.

All together these prayers make up one decade.

After the completion of the five mysteries (five decades), the 'Hail Holy Queen' is said:

Hail, holy queen, mother of mercy, our life, our sweetness, and our hope. To thee do we cry, poor banished children of Eve. To thee do we send up our sighs, mourning and weeping in this valley of tears. Turn then, most gracious advocate, thine eyes of mercy towards us, and after this our exile show us the blessed fruit of thy womb, Jesus. O clement, O loving, O sweet Virgin Mary.

Pray for us, O holy mother of God.

That we may be made worthy of the promises of Christ.

Let us pray.

O God whose only begotten Son by his life, death and resurrection has obtained for us the rewards of eternal salvation, grant we beseech thee that by meditating upon the mysteries of the most holy Rosary of the most Blessed Virgin Mary we may imitate what they contain and obtain what they promise through the same Christ our Lord.

Amen

Conclusion

'May the Lord give you peace!'

This was the greeting that St Francis wanted the brothers to begin and end every conversation with. He spoke of it as the greeting that God had given him to give to the earth. I cherish it as a reminder that God wants us to be at peace, lovingly desires it for us and wants all of us to carry this peace in our own hearts first and then from our hearts to every being we meet. Peace in the contemplative sense is not just the absence of conflict but the deep Divine *shalom*, the peace that allows me to live in right relationship with God, with myself and with every other being. It is a choice as much as a gift.

I hope that this little book has given you moments, still points, of this peace, or at least allowed you to discover again the possibility of dwelling in that peace that passes all understanding, which lies at the heart of all creation and is always at the deepest still point of your soul. This peace restores us, heals us and allows us to become who we were always meant to be. When we live with mindful awareness and walk the contemplative path, we become instruments of that peace.

To live from that peaceful centre does not mean that we won't face times of pain and sadness and turmoil, but it does mean that we will understand that those times will come and go, no matter how long it takes, and that, beneath and behind them, there is always a foundation of unconquerable peace, a still, small voice of love, a sacred union that calls us into the depths of love, love for all our fellow creatures and the Divine Love in which we live and move and have our being.

Whether you have followed the book through the year, used it from time to time or are returning to it after a long time away, remember that you are loved, that new beginning is always possible in each succeeding present moment, and that the one who is love desires only that you are at peace.

May St Francis dance through the streets of your heart, draw you into mindful, meditative brother/sisterhood with all that lives, and sing his song of peace in the still point of your soul.

'The Lord give you peace!'

Lockdown

Yes there is fear.
Yes there is isolation.
Yes there is panic-buying.
Yes there is sickness.
Yes there is even death.
But,
They say that in Wuhan after so many years of noise
You can hear the birds again.
They say that after just a few weeks of quiet
The sky is no longer thick with fumes
But blue and grey and clear.
They say that in the streets of Assisi
People are singing to each other
Across the empty squares,
Keeping their windows open
So that those who are alone
May hear the sounds of family around them.
They say that a hotel in the west of Ireland
Is offering free meals and delivery to the housebound.
Today a young woman I know
Is busy spreading fliers with her number
Through the neighbourhood
So that the elders may have someone to call on.
Today churches, synagogues, mosques and temples
Are preparing to welcome
And shelter the homeless, the sick, the weary.
All over the world people are slowing down and reflecting.
All over the world people are looking at their neighbours
in a new way.

All over the world people are waking up to a new reality.
To how big we really are.
To how little control we really have.
To what really matters.
To love.
So we pray and we remember that
Yes there is fear.
But there does not have to be hate.
Yes there is isolation.
But there does not have to be loneliness.
Yes there is panic-buying.
But there does not have to be meanness.
Yes there is sickness.
But there does not have to be disease of the soul.
Yes there is even death.
But there can always be a rebirth of love.
Wake to the choices you make as to how to live now.
Today, breathe.
Listen, behind the factory noises of your panic
The birds are singing again,
The sky is clearing,
Spring is coming,
And we are always encompassed by love.
Open the windows of your soul
And though you may not be able
To touch across the empty square,
Sing.

13 March 2020

The Little Poem with the Long Legs

The book you are holding exists because of a little poem – 'Lockdown'. Right at the start of the pandemic, while we watched the world close down around us, and just as Ireland was facing its first, frightening moment of having to make restrictions for the safety of her people, this little poem came to me all in one rush of grace and gift. I put it out into the world on Facebook and then went to bed. I woke to a phone exploding with notifications and the shock of watching these few lines run off into the world … I could not have imagined how far it would travel.

Since then, it has been around the world many times, been read aloud and shared by millions, including royals and celebrities, pop stars and government ministers, translated (at last count) into 28 languages and inspired three short films, four animated retellings and many, many musical versions ranging from folk to dance to full chorale and so much art …

The poem took my breath away and still does … not because of its going viral … but because it showed me just how much we are all craving for meaning, for stillness, for peace. 'Lockdown' reminded me as it came and others who read it when it came to them that where meditation, prayer and deep awareness are then no matter how difficult, tragic and painful our circumstances are we can always find moments of beauty around us, we can always be a good neighbour and that we are always encompassed by love.

Contemplative Lexicon of Words Used in the Text

agios pneumatikos	holy breath/ Holy Spirit
apophatic	the way of silence before the mystery that is God
ascesis	strict self-discipline
Deus meus et omnia	my God and my all
kavannah	mindfulness (attentiveness of the heart)
lectio divina	the meditative reading of scripture
logisimoi	distracting thoughts
mandatum novum	new commandment
mantra	sacred utterance *or* phrase
metanoia	conversion ('returning' or 'turning again' to God)
na'avi	prophet (one who sees deeply)
nephesh	soul
Nunc Dimittus	now dismiss (the first two words in Latin from the Canticle of Simeon in the Gospel of Luke. Has the sense of a life now complete)
pax et bonum	peace and joyful goodness
pneuma	breath of life
prosekai	mindfully aware
ruach	the spirit of God within us, also a word for breath and life in Hebrew
shalom	peace
transitus	passing into eternal life
versiculum	prayer word

Acknowledgements

The danger of saying thanks is always that someone may feel left out – nonetheless I will try! If you do feel forgotten, I beg your forgiveness and please know that no one was excluded deliberately but only through the fallibility that affects all who make this human journey.

So, with a deep bow of thanks to one and all, I begin.

To the Lady, my Queen to whom my whole life is dedicated, though very unworthily, I offer my deepest thanks. Whatever inspiration exists in these pages came as a gift from you.

To the ancient and wonderful family of Francis and Clare, for all you've taught me and for all you've done for me, I thank you and, in the same breath, apologise for being such a poor representative of the way of peace and joy you incarnate in the world.

To my family, I have no words to express what you all mean to me. To render me silent is no doubt a gift to you all. But especially to my dad, Richard; to my late and most wonderful mother, Marion; to my brothers and sister, David, John and Anne Marie, you always have my deepest thanks and blessings for all you are, and all you teach me every day.

To Sharon, who has walked the path with me for so long, I offer the deepest and most profound thanks for being, simply and wonderfully, who you are. You have been soul friend, teacher, advisor and, so often, navigator when I am lost! There are no words – I simply bow and ask pardon for my many failings on the way.

To all my friends who have walked with me at different times and in different ways. Thank you for your teaching and for the privilege of your company.

To all in the Sanctuary Centre in Dublin: to Sister Stan, Sister Síle, Niamh, Jane and Tony – thank you for sharing the practice, inviting me to teach and willing this book into being in so many ways.

To Sister Stan and Michael Harding for their kind words about this book, and to Ciara Doorley and her team in Hachette Ireland for all the work done in making this book a reality.

To all those of all the communities of practice and all faiths that have inspired me and helped me on the way, whether online or in real life.

To the trees and stones and deep ancient beings of Marlay, Ards, Assisi, Axladitsa and Avalon and all the sacred and holy teachers of earth and sky – a bow of gratitude and reverence.

Finally to the ancestors: to my Gran, who taught me to see deeply, and Brother John who invited me to listen closely and to Father H who taught me everyone is a child of grace. I offer to you and to all the deepest bow of reverence and gratitude.